BOSTON COLLEGE
Morrissey College of Arts and Sciences

FROM BEIRUT TO BELFAST
HOW POWER-SHARING ARRANGEMENTS AFFECT
ETHNIC TENSIONS IN POST-CONFLICT SOCIETIES

By

Czar Alexei Sepe

Advised by Professor Peter Krause, Ph.D.

An Honors Senior Thesis submitted to The Honors
Program of the Department of Political Science

FROM BEIRUT TO BELFAST

HOW POWER-SHARING ARRANGEMENTS AFFECT
ETHNIC TENSIONS IN POST-CONFLICT SOCIETIES

CZAR ALEXEI SEPE

authorHOUSE

AuthorHouse™
1663 Liberty Drive
Bloomington, IN 47403
www.authorhouse.com
Phone: 833-262-8899

Published by AuthorHouse 06/11/2021

ISBN: 978-1-6655-2767-5 (sc)
ISBN: 978-1-6655-2766-8 (e)

Print information available on the last page.

Any people depicted in stock imagery provided by Getty Images are models, and such images are being used for illustrative purposes only.
Certain stock imagery © Getty Images.

This book is printed on acid-free paper.

Because of the dynamic nature of the Internet, any web addresses or links contained in this book may have changed since publication and may no longer be valid. The views expressed in this work are solely those of the author and do not necessarily reflect the views of the publisher, and the publisher hereby disclaims any responsibility for them.

Dedicated to my aunt, Mary Jane Mercado, who lost her life to COVID-19, and to all healthcare heroes fighting against the Coronavirus pandemic at the time of this writing.

CONTENTS

TABLE OF FIGURES

PREFACE AND ACKNOWLEDGEMENTS

I was sitting on my AerLingus flight from Dublin to Newark, reminiscing—as any college student who studies abroad does—of the memories I've made during my semester in Ireland. Scrolling through my Facebook timeline, I reflected on the weekend excursions, the nightly outings, and the new friends I made. I can safely say I enjoyed the good *craic.*

One photo stuck out to me.

In October 2019, I visited Northern Ireland for a couple of days. I had only learned tidbits of the political turbulence that roiled that part of the island, like the notorious IRA or Bloody Sunday (which was just a U2 song to me then). I recalled encountering a protest in front of Belfast City Hall. The protestors kindly informed me that they were upset because the city hall stopped flying the Union Jack in 2012. Frankly, the demonstration felt more like the monthly meeting at your local Elks Lodge: about 10 people, all pretty old, holding up their little flags and signs as they talk about the 'good ol' days.' But the flags they were waving were extremely provocative if you knew what they meant. It was the regimental colors of the 1st Battalion, Parachute Regiment—the British soldiers who perpetrated the Bloody Sunday massacre. In a ludicrous photo, I stand in front of the protestors: thumbs-up, smiling obliviously. Just like your stereotypical tourist.

The summer beforehand, I was in Beirut, and the parallels were uncanny. Thanks to the Aggad Fellowship, I studied beginner Arabic at the Lebanese American University. Sectarianism felt so blatant in Lebanon. Meandering throughout the cluttered streets, I saw political posters everywhere, depicting politicians with their eye-to-eye grins—but there wasn't even an election going on. Walking through an alleyway from the grocery store to my apartment, I saw a group of older men, about 5 of them, towards the end of the street. They sat around in a circle with their plastic chairs, sipping their coffee and smoking their hookahs. Next to them was the sky-blue flag of the Future Movement, a Sunni political party. As I passed them, they all perked up, mumbling to each other—serving as sentinels for their neighborhood. Visibly shaken, I scurry off, avoiding their menacing glares. Safe to say, I did *not* take a picture with them.

For me, this symbolic parallel commenced my rabbit-hole exploration of the similarities between Lebanon and Northern Ireland. Both countries have confessional governments. Both experienced internal political strife; both were bloody and fratricidal. Both countries were known as notorious havens for terrorism. However, I felt one intuitive difference: Lebanon felt like a nation in disarray, unable to cope with its civil war past (I was there three months before the October Revolution), while Northern Ireland felt lively and hopeful for their future. In one place, I can jokingly take a picture with the Loyalist partisans—in the other, I felt like I was going to get into some serious trouble with a Sunni gang. Why?

My thesis is an attempt to answer the questions I raised during my time abroad. It also gave me a good excuse to look back on my own 'good ol' days' in Europe and the Middle East, especially since foreign travel won't be occurring in the near future. Most importantly, though, it serves to showcase how I've developed as a writer and researcher, both in history and political science. Though cliché, I really do believe this work is a culmination of my undergraduate academic career. To this end, I should thank a few people who've helped me along the way.

Inspiration for the title came from Thomas Friedman's award-winning memoir, *From Beirut to Jerusalem* (1989). In the off-chance you ever stumble upon this thesis, Mr. Friedman, I must say thank you.

I was lucky enough to make many friends in Dublin and Beirut. To my Irish friends: thank you for sharing your candid thoughts with me. I would like to particularly thank Séan Quinn at Trinity College, Dublin, for recommending that I visit Belfast. Alongside great hummus and plenty of sun, I must thank my Lebanese friends for giving me valuable insight: Joe Monem, John Haibi, Raed Khairallah and Firas Farah. Special thanks go to LAU's SINARC program and my Arabic teachers: Laure Obeid and Sara Ammar. Also, I must thank Ghia from the Université Saint Joseph for our Global Conversations discussion, as she shed light on her country's situation. My heart goes out to Lebanon—for its suffering, but resilient people.

I must thank my thesis advisor, Professor Peter Krause, and the department thesis supervisor, Professor Jennie Purnell. Working with

Prof. Krause on his research team sophomore year exposed me to research methods and political violence literature—but most importantly, he fostered my keen interest in this field. So during the end of my junior year, I felt it was a no-brainer to ask him to advise me. Prof. Krause has been *very* patient with me throughout the writing process. And I have learned many lessons, from overcoming methodological roadblocks to making some of the most stunning scholarly figures you've ever seen. I hope you enjoy reading all of this, Professor. Many thanks also go to Prof. Purnell, who was flexible as I decided to push on writing this work, in a time when I had personally felt overwhelmed during the pandemic. My thanks also go to librarian Julia Hughes, who guided me through primary source databases and procured books I requested that supplemented my research.

I would like to thank the Boston College community for their support, pushing me to do bigger and better things, and fostering my intellectual and social life. I must thank my mentors: Professor Kathleen Bailey, Professor Oliver Rafferty, S.J., Professor Robert Savage, and Monetta Edwards, Director of the Winston Center for Leadership and Ethics. They always had their door open to me whenever I needed advice, pushing me in various directions and providing me with immense opportunities. My Perspectives teacher, Professor Antonia Atanassova, deserves my thanks as well. She gave me the confidence and encouragement to publish an essay in an undergraduate journal freshman year, fostering my academic curiosity in Stokes Hall. My thanks go out to my friends at BC, especially my roommates: the 'Sleepover,' 'Rubi' D41 and D42, and the 'Kirkwood Manor' boys. May Route 66 live on. Special thanks go to Thomas Shade, whose mastery of tables guided my work.

Lastly, I must thank my friends and family in Parsippany, New Jersey. To my mom, dad, and *lola*: I know I gave you all a heart attack when I said I was going to Beirut. Nevertheless, thank you for your tireless support for everything I do—and above all, for your unbounded love.

C. A. Sepe
Chestnut Hill, MA
April 2, 2021

CHAPTER 1

INTRODUCTION: POWER-SHARING THROUGH THE REARVIEW WINDOW?

*"My friends and my road-fellows, pity the nation
that is full of beliefs and empty of religion.
Pity the nation that wears a cloth it does not weave, eats bread it does not
harvest, and drinks a wine that flows not from its own winepress…"
"Pity the nation whose sages are dumb with years
and whose strong men are yet in the cradle.
Pity the nation divided into fragments, each
fragment deeming itself a nation."*

– Kahlil Gibran, *The Garden of the Prophet*[1]

*"History says, Don't hope / On the side of the grave,' / But
then, once in a lifetime / The longed for tidal wave / Of
justice can rise up / And hope and history rhyme."
"So hope for a great sea-change / On the far side of revenge.
/ Believe that a further shore / Is reachable from here. /
Believe in miracles. / And cures and healing wells."*

– Seamus Heaney, *The Cure of Troy*[2]

1.1: *Introduction*

If you have the chance to go to Beirut, don't take an Uber—take
a *service* (pronounced *"ser-vees"*). These decades-old sedans meander

---

[1] "The Garden Of The Prophet by Kahlil Gibran," accessed February 24, 2021,
http://gutenberg.net.au/ebooks05/0500581h.html.
[2] "The Cure of Troy," *Pittsburgh Post-Gazette*, accessed March 24, 2021, https://www.
post-gazette.com/news/insight/2021/02/21/The-cure-of-Troy/stories/202102210026.

throughout the city, clogging up the congested main arteries built over ancient Roman roads, honking and heckling their way to make a living. Standard fare is usually LL2,000—a little over $1 USD—for almost anywhere in the greater Beirut area, but as custom, you'll have to negotiate with your taxi driver.[3] There is one caveat though: as Nayla Assaf writes, drivers like Abu George "would not settle for less than LL7,000 to take his customer from Gemaizeh to Caracas, a distance that could be covered in 15 minutes providing there [was] no other traffic."[4] On the other hand, a trip from Gemaizeh to Hazmiyeh, which is a further distance, only costs the standard LL2,000.[5] Abu George is not being absurd or nonsensical—it's the norm.

In reality, this is a recurring pattern among many *service* drivers. It is a subtle remnant of Lebanon's civil war, which separated East and West Beirut between Christians and Muslims, respectively. Driving from Gemaizeh to Caracas involves crossing the dividing line—the notorious 'Green Line'—but not Gemaizeh to Hazmiyeh, neighborhoods that both lie in East Beirut. Assaf puts it eloquently: "Although the barricades, the checkpoints and the militiamen once positioned on either side of the three demarcation lines disappeared…after the 1975-1990 civil war ended, in most taxi drivers' minds, they are still there."[6] The ghost of the Green Line lingers, and the mental barriers emanate throughout everyday life in Beirut.

---

[3] This was the case when I visited Lebanon in June and July 2019. Since the financial collapse in the autumn of that year, the country has hit hyperinflation. For decades, the Lebanese pound was pegged at "roughly 1,500 to the dollar," however, "dollars were being sold on the black market for up to L£9,500." In real terms, the "average prices for food and non-alcoholic beverages rose 402 per cent" in one year alone. See Chloe Cornish, "Currency Crisis Leaves Lebanese Cupboards Bare," *Financial Times*, February 21, 2021, https://www.ft.com/content/69e1e040-d8d7-494e-9a90-6f02f68f0bf7.

[4] "Green Line Lives on in Minds of Beirut's Taxi Drivers," *The Daily Star Newspaper - Lebanon*, October 13, 2003, https://www.dailystar.com.lb//News/Lebanon-News/2003/Oct-13/40396-green-line-lives-on-in-minds-of-beiruts-taxi-drivers.ashx.

[5] Ibid. Assaf's report, written in 2003, says the standard *service* fare was LL1,000. From personal experience, the fare has since increased to LL2,000 (as of July 2019).

[6] Ibid.

Speaking to another *service* driver, Richard Hall interviews Gabriel Saad about conversation etiquette: "politics is off the table, [Saad] adds—it's too divisive. But bemoaning the state of the country is the great unifier."[7] Lebanon is approaching thirty years since the end of its civil war, but even after all that time, the war's zeitgeist stubbornly persists. The *services* themselves, a system created when the civil war decimated the country's public transportation, have survived sectarian strife, foreign occupation, and Islamist terrorism. It does help that the Lebanese state has been incapable of rebuilding the public transport system since the 1989 Taif Accords that ushered in peace. What unifies the Lebanese people, ironically, is Saad's sentiments, embodied in the common expression: *hukoomi zift*. Translated literally to "the government is asphalt," the word *zift* is an insult in Arabic, so a better translation would go along the lines of "the government is shit."[8]

Unfortunately, Lebanon is in an abysmal state. Since anti-government protests rocked Beirut in October 2019, a banking and political crisis precipitated, devaluating the Lebanese pound and ruining the savings of many people—all on top of the Coronavirus pandemic. A year later, government ineptitude culminated in the August 2020 Beirut port explosion, when "nearly 3,000 tons of ammonium nitrate detonated, killed 211 people and injured more than 6,000."[9] An influx of global sympathy and solidarity after the blast projected Lebanon's plight on the world stage. Nonetheless, international aid is being conditioned on wholesale government reforms, but negotiations over power-sharing Cabinet positions

---

[7] "Uber Has Met Its Match with Lebanon's Old-School Carpool Taxis," *The World from PRX*, accessed February 26, 2021, https://www.pri.org/stories/2017-11-03/city-s-cheap-old-school-carpool-service-puts-uber-test.

[8] See "How Do You Translate 'Zeft'?," *ArabLit & ArabLit Quarterly*, accessed February 27, 2021, https://arablit.org/2016/08/26/how-do-you-translate-zeft/. This article provides a lively discussion on the meanings and connotations of the word *zift*. A debate about how to effectively convey the meaning of the word into English ensued after the prominent Arab commentator Sultan Sooud al-Qassemi asked for a translation on his Facebook page.

[9] "Protests in Lebanon as Local Currency Hits Record Low," *AP News*, accessed March 4, 2021, https://apnews.com/article/lebanon-coronavirus-pandemic-financial-markets-syria-beirut-68f65031f2a987ca52f483c74e50593f.

are at a deadlock (as of March 2021). Because of these cascading crises, the World Bank asserts that Lebanon is faced with "an arduous and prolonged depression."[10] Hala Saghbini's Tweet captures the national mood: "The dollar is equal to 10,000 pounds. People are hungry, prices are flying and there is no electricity. We want a government immediately. Enough humiliation of the people."[11] Although this spiral of tragedy is enveloping the country, you can count on one thing: the *service* will live on, zigzagging Beirut—its taxi drivers providing an integral lifeline for the nation.

Meanwhile, in a different part of the world, taking a taxi becomes a history lesson—and yes, even a tourist attraction. These are the Black Taxis of Belfast. Taxi drivers operate tours through East and West Belfast for mesmerized foreigners—many of whom are spending a weekend around Northern Ireland's luscious countryside and natural landmarks, like the Giants' Causeway. The drivers are not only your tour guides, but in keeping with the island's poetic tradition, they transform into wise Irish bards who recount harrowing tales of violence, hatred, and sectarian revenge. Driving you past one of the over sixty "peace walls," they point to the murals that adorn the barriers dividing Catholic and Protestant communities.[12] The artwork illustrates a troubled past, but also a hopeful future. As one mural says, "there's more in common…than what divides us."[13] I took one of these tours in the fall of 2019. When I asked if Guinness (which is a pub staple in the Republic of Ireland) is ubiquitous among the Northern Irish regardless of sectarian affiliation, David, our driver, first hesitated—then responded: "Does a bear shit in the woods?"

The tourism sector has played a key role in the reconciliation process in Northern Ireland, providing new economic opportunities for its people. The Troubles, an ethnic-religious conflict that ravaged the region for over thirty years, was thrust into global consciousness when the BBC

---

[10] Ibid.

[11] Ibid.

[12] "The Peace Walls of Belfast: Do They Still Help Keep the Keep the Peace?," *CBC*, August 29, 2019, https://www.cbc.ca/radio/ideas/the-peace-walls-of-belfast-do-they-still-help-keep-the-peace-1.5262640.

[13] Hugh Biggar, "The Murals on Belfast's 'Peace Walls' Offer an Illustrated History of the Troubles," *Washington Post*, accessed March 4, 2021, https://www.washingtonpost.com/lifestyle/travel/the-murals-on-belfasts-peace-walls-offer-an-illustrated-history-of-the-troubles/2018/08/15/4c993480-9cca-11e8-8d5e-c6c594024954_story.html.

broadcasted brutal images of innocent protestors being gunned down in the street by the British army—an event known as Bloody Sunday.[14] Today, streams of tourists gawk at working-class Belfast neighborhoods most affected by the political violence: places like the Falls Road and the Short Strand. This "dark tourism," or the "desire to visit places worldwide which are linked to atrocities and tragedies," has been a worldwide trend in recent years—and the Northern Irish have cashed in on it.[15] In 2001, only three years after the signing of the 1998 Belfast Agreement (commonly known as the Good Friday Agreement), "the six counties that comprise the province drew 1.2 million visitors…and a solid percentage of them are drawn to the place by a fascination with the Northern Ireland of the headlines."[16] By 2019, the province drew a whopping 5.3 million visitors and about £1 billion into the local economy.[17] It seems that Northern Ireland has overcome its divisions, and can even share its historical pains to the world as an avenue for economic growth.

But of course, it's not that simple. For its part, Northern Ireland has maintained peace—albeit a tense, frigid one. The 2016 Brexit referendum renewed concerns for ethnic violence in the province. The main problem for Northern Ireland was the imposition of hard border checks between north and south on the island—thereby violating the peace agreement—if the UK were to withdraw from the EU Common Market. Republicans capitalized on majority discontent over the Brexit result and reinvigorated

---

[14] See Robert J. Savage, *The BBC's "Irish Troubles": Television, Conflict and Northern Ireland* (Manchester: University Press, 2015), 93-5. Savage writes how the iconic footage of Father Edward Daly carrying a gunned-down youth was a diplomatic fiasco for the British. For example, after those images were transmitted across the Atlantic, the British embassy in Washington frantically went into damage control—especially in light of the outcry from prominent Irish-American members of Congress, like Senator Ted Kennedy.

[15] "'Dark Tourism' Booms at Northern Ireland's Troubles Museums," *BBC News*, accessed March 4, 2021, https://www.bbc.com/news/uk-northern-ireland-46046674.

[16] Tom Mudd, "In Belfast, Cabs Offer Tours Showing Scenes of Conflict," *Wall Street Journal*, May 24, 2002, https://www.wsj.com/articles/SB1022159743471097240.

[17] "Tourism | Department for the Economy," May 17, 2015, https://www.economy-ni.gov.uk/topics/tourism; "The Tourist Economy in Northern Ireland," accessed March 4, 2021, https://www.nibusinessinfo.co.uk/content/tourist-economy-northern-ireland.

calls for a border poll with the goal of Irish unification.[18] Yet, in 2017, Sinn Féin exited power-sharing, and the country was left without a regional government. After a three-year hiatus from Stormont, Sinn Féin (SF) and the Democratic Unionist Party (DUP) entered into power-sharing in January 2020, enacting a compromise deal that revised institutional procedures and finally acknowledged the Irish language (alongside the Ulster-Scots language)—just before the Coronavirus pandemic.[19] Nonetheless, trouble looms on the horizon. In March 2021, a council of loyalist paramilitary groups renounced the Good Friday Agreement (GFA) because of the Northern Ireland protocol in the UK-EU trade deal.[20] Political tensions are rising, and ethnic animosities are re-awakening, but as the debate rages on, the Black Taxis idly stand by in Belfast city center amidst worldwide travel bans—waiting for their longed-for tourists.

This tale of two taxis magnifies broader, deep-rooted questions about war, peace, and reconciliation—in parts of the world where sectarian division has been a way of life. Lebanon and Northern Ireland are examples of what scholars have termed as "deeply divided societies": "post-war countries with salient vertical (identity-based) cleavages that are perceived to threaten stability and peace," according to Rima Majed.[21] In the wake of post-World War II decolonization and the era of national liberation movements, questions about nationhood and identity challenged theorists and practitioners alike. Since the fall of the Soviet Union, renewed attention to ethnic violence captured political scientists and the general public. As the world watched in horror the atrocities at Srebrenica and

---

[18] Gerry Moriarty, "Shared Island: Northern Ireland Is Still a Society on a Sectarian Edge," *The Irish Times*, accessed February 22, 2021, https://www.irishtimes.com/news/ireland/irish-news/shared-island-northern-ireland-is-still-a-society-on-a-sectarian-edge-1.4344699.

[19] "Stormont Talks: Main NI Parties Agree Power-Sharing Deal," *BBC News*, January 10, 2020, https://www.bbc.com/news/uk-northern-ireland-51068774.

[20] "Brexit: Loyalist Paramilitary Groups Renounce Good Friday Agreement," *The Guardian*, March 4, 2021, http://www.theguardian.com/uk-news/2021/mar/04/brexit-northern-ireland-loyalist-armies-renounce-good-friday-agreement.

[21] Rima Majed, "What's So Deep About Deeply Divided Societies? Rethinking Sectarianism in the Middle East," *American University of Beirut*, accessed February 27, 2021, http://www.aub.edu.lb:80/nyo/Briefings/Pages/sectarianismfulltextsummary.aspx.

Rwanda—seemingly 'tribe-like,' 'primordial,' and hate-fueled genocides and massacres—fierce debates over the United States' "responsibility to protect" (R2P) engulfed Washington.[22] Conflict resolution theories endeavored to find political and institutional solutions to deep-rooted conflict in these societies. This is where the concept of 'power-sharing' comes in.

Power-sharing institutions—or consociationalism—are, as Caroline Hartzell and Matthew Hoddie define, "rules that, in addition to defining how decisions will be made by groups within the polity, allocate decision-making rights, including access to state resources, among collectivities competing for power."[23] These specific arrangements, comprised of special constitutions, electoral processes, and safeguards were seen by many as a political path towards peace in divided societies. From apartheid South Africa to the minuscule island of Bougainville, political leaders devised power-sharing frameworks that account for opposing ethnic communities. Indeed, the constitutional make-ups of Lebanon and Northern Ireland are viewed as consociationalism *par excellence*. Both countries were involved in violent political conflicts between ethnic-religious communities and ended their hostilities via power-sharing. Both polities have maintained power-sharing institutions since the end of the twentieth century. However, how has power-sharing played out in these two countries, and many other divided societies, after peace is achieved? I had a hunch that there must be some relationship between Lebanon's absolute failure as a state and Northern Ireland's relative success. Why is this the case?

My thesis picks up the conversation on this topic. Recent literature has explored power-sharing in practice, and the successes and challenges states have faced when implementing this form of constitution. How have power-sharing institutions affected divided societies? What effects have they had on ethnic identities? Why do some arrangements succeed, while others fail? A lively debate about the answers to these questions has kept the

---

[22] See Charles Homans, "Responsibility to Protect: A Short History," *Foreign Policy*, October 11, 2011, https://foreignpolicy.com/2011/10/11/responsibility-to-protect-a-short-history/.

[23] Caroline A Hartzell and Matthew Hoddie, "Power Sharing and the Rule of Law in the Aftermath of Civil War," *International Studies Quarterly* 63, no. 3 (September 1, 2019): 641–53, https://doi.org/10.1093/isq/sqz023, 643.

fields of conflict resolution and ethnic violence interesting and engaging. As I studied these subjects, I was intrigued by a particular facet in this debate; namely, questions about the relationship between power-sharing arrangements and ethnic tensions. Thus, I decided to ask, "To what extent do power-sharing institutions affect ethnic tensions in divided societies?" In the following chapters, I attempt to find some answers.

1.2: *Thesis Outline*

To what extent do power-sharing arrangements increase or decrease ethnic tensions? How can we conceptualize a way to analyze power-sharing that better reflects its potential effects on ethnic animosities? Why do power-sharing agreements succeed or fail? This thesis sets to explore these questions through a theoretical framework that will help analyze post-conflict societies. Using Lebanon and Northern Ireland as comparative case studies, I test my theoretical framework to see if it can provide a potential explanation of the relationship between power-sharing and ethnic tensions (if there is any). I provide key insights for academics and practitioners on power-sharing institutions, weighing their merits and limitations through my conceptual lens.

In Chapter 2, I lay a foundation to understand power-sharing agreements in relation to ethnic tensions in post-conflict societies. To better conceptualize the research question, I separate it into two main parts: political institutions and ethnic identity. I provide a literature review of conflict resolution theories, zeroing in on consociational theories of democracy. Then, I engage in theories of ethnicity and identity formation, using scholarly works from historians, anthropologists, and social scientists to answer this fundamental question: "what is ethnicity?" To sum up, I find that ethnic identity is not primordial nor static. Rather it is developed and constantly reconfigured in relation to others, creating an in-group/out-group dynamic via an actual or perceived common blood lineage. Ethnicity is not inherently political, but in ethnically divided countries, it becomes *the* main political cleavage.

With these concepts identified, defined, and operationalized, I present my theory of power-sharing and ethnic tensions. I use Pierre Nora's *lieux de mémoire* scheme of historical memory to craft a theory of sites of social interaction (SSIs for short). Three sites of social interaction are (1) sites of contestation, where interactions are a zero-sum game, resulting in winners and losers; (2) sites of coexistence, where interactions are underpinned by a notion of tolerance or a 'stay-in-your-own-lane' mentality; and (3) sites of collaboration, where interactions are of mutual benefit, and separate identities share the space. In addition, I outline three main strategies of social cohesion in power-sharing institutions to supplement my analysis of ethnic tensions, namely: (1) assimilation, in which a new national identity is constructed or a hegemonic ethnic identity is imposed on all other ethnic groups; (2) differentiation, in which ethnic identities are tolerated in society and a pluralistic outlook takes root; and (3) segregation, in which ethnic groups are separated, causing a bifurcation of national identity. These predictions inform my final hypothesis: SSIs and cohesion strategies that increase tensions will cause power-sharing failure in the long run, and vice versa—SSIs and cohesion strategies that decrease tensions will lead to power-sharing success.

In theory, certain sites of social interaction and cohesion strategies will increase or decrease ethnic tensions. Sites of contestation are more likely to increase tensions, while sites of collaboration may decrease tensions. A strategy of assimilation is conducive to an increase in ethnic antagonisms, while segregation is conducive to a corresponding decrease. Both sites of coexistence and a differentiation strategy may either increase or decrease ethnic tensions, depending on case-specific factors. All these logics are spelled out in Chapter 2, giving us ample material to test in our two case studies: Lebanon and Northern Ireland. The research design consists of a structured, focused comparison combined with smaller within-case studies. I provide historical context and process trace the practice of power-sharing in both polities, to inform my textual analysis of the Taif Accords and the Belfast Agreement. I premise my empirical chapters on the congruence method to see whether or not my hypotheses stand up to scrutiny in the Lebanon and Northern Ireland cases by conducting within-case analyses of particular aspects of society.

Chapters 3 and 4 engage in each case's power-sharing arrangements, their implementation, and specific areas of post-conflict society within the SSI and cohesion strategy framework. In the third chapter, I explore the case of Lebanon. I trace Lebanon's history of power-sharing, noting how consociation has been an integral institution for the country, to keep the mosaic of ethnic and religious communities in harmony. Ethnic tensions rose drastically in the aftermath of Lebanese independence and the Palestinian national movement, which brought about the Lebanese civil war in 1975. About fifteen years later in 1989, ethnic-religious paramilitary groups were ready—with the looming shadow of Syria—to enter into peace negotiations, culminating in the Taif Accords.

I then study the power-sharing structures in Taif, placing its provisions in the theory of sites of social interaction and cohesion strategies. The settlement was clearly designed to placate multiple ethnic-group actors, which resulted in divergent SSIs and cohesion strategies throughout the document. I conclude that in its general outlook, the Taif Accords envisioned a site of coexistence and pursued assimilation and differentiation strategies. In engaging with two specific spheres in Taif—Lebanese education and economic segregation/displacement—I determine the extent to which the treaty was implemented, and if these sites and strategies were manifested as envisioned in the settlement. Due to many factors, such as Syrian interference, the power-sharing agreement was only somewhat implemented. This is expressed in both cases of Lebanese education and economic/war displacement, as these post-war spheres became sites of contestation through political corruption, clientelism, the meddling of the religious lobby, and the neoliberal economic program that catered to the wealthy, rather than the majority of Lebanese society. I gauge ethnic sentiments, concluding that there has been a substantial increase in sectarian animosities since 1989. Lebanon is indicative of the pitfalls of the SSIs and cohesion strategies outlined on paper and their implementation in society. Due to these discrepancies, sectarian animosities are exasperated. Therefore, I find that my hypotheses correspond to Lebanon's post-war regime—and its failure.

The fourth chapter analyzes Northern Ireland. Unlike Lebanon, Northern Ireland does not have a legacy of power-sharing. The formation of Northern Ireland ensured a Protestant-majority regime. For its first forty years, Protestants held a solid grip over the country. However, Irish Catholic nationalists, mobilized along ethnic-religious lines, overwhelmed the Protestant unionist Stormont government in the wake of the civil rights protests, in the late 1960s. By 1972, paramilitary groups engaged in political violence, commencing the Troubles. After failed attempts at resolving the political issues that fomented the violence in the region—from the 1973 Sunningdale Agreement to the 1985 Anglo-Irish Agreement—the United Kingdom, the Republic of Ireland, and Northern Irish parties reached the 1998 Belfast Agreement (Good Friday Agreement). I analyze this power-sharing agreement, which contains a multidimensional approach and focuses not only on political institutions but cultural and socio-economic issues too.

I discern an overarching SSIs of coexistence and collaboration, as well as a strategy of differentiation, in the Northern Irish power-sharing agreement. The parity of esteem, a normative concept that called for the equality of group status throughout society, undergirded the GFA—thereby instilling sites of coexistence and collaboration through differentiation. Similar to the Lebanese case, I conduct an in-depth study, using our established theories, of two provisions included in the GFA: anti-discrimination and employment equality, and decommissioning. On balance, the anti-discrimination and equality efforts were successfully implemented, resulting in sites of coexistence and collaboration in the workforce and creating differentiation. The decommissioning issue transitioned between SSIs during the scope of my investigation: envisioned as a collaborative SSI, it quickly became a site of contestation, until the IRA fully dumped arms. So, in this case, the result was a site of coexistence through an assimilation strategy. My analysis of polling data proves that ethnic tensions have slightly decreased since 1998. Thus, I find congruence in my hypothesis for the Northern Irish case study—proving that SSIs, cohesion strategies, and ethnic tensions all have an important causal link to the success or failure of a power-sharing regime after peace is achieved.

In Chapter 5, I present my overall conclusions, provide implications, ask new questions, and present my final remarks about this thesis. There is a clear causal link between power-sharing arrangements and ethnic tensions in divided societies, through the mechanisms of SSIs and cohesion strategies. Power-sharing outcomes are dependent on ethnic tensions. If tensions increase, due to SSIs and cohesion strategies that correspond to an increase in animosities, the power-sharing regime will fail. Conversely, power-sharing succeeds when tensions decrease, because of SSIs and cohesion strategies that were suited to decrease tensions. Lebanon and

Northern Ireland encode power-sharing institutions with different sites of social interaction, as a reflection of a society's composition, and different cohesion strategies, as a reflection of power-sharing design. Implementation, I conclude, provides us with the missing link in our knowledge of power-sharing and ethnic tensions. My theory of society, institutional design, and ethnic identity expresses these mechanisms and logics, to explain why power-sharing does, or does not, work.

1.3: *Power-Sharing Through the Rearview Window?*

In our tale of two taxis, we see Abu George and David navigate the ghosts of a post-war environment in different ways. While the Beiruti *service* driver would hike up your fare for crossing the invisible sectarian dividing line due to the risks, the Belfast cab driver (who identifies as a Protestant) had no qualms showing us a mural of Bobby Sands in the republican Falls Road neighborhood. Lebanon and Northern Ireland, once notorious for political violence and terrorism, have achieved peace. But what kind of peace? Is peace avoiding neighborhoods of differing sectarian affiliation? Is peace commercializing ethnic tensions and an unsettled past? It is clear that power-sharing has a tangible, real effect on the lives of everyday people in these societies. Whether it is Taif or Good Friday, Beirut or Belfast, the grand institutions and hopes that power-sharing once held have given way to practical, sobering realities. This is a unique moment in time, because there is enough distance to try to study the effects of power-sharing with a degree of objectivity, yet it is close enough that many people hold deeply-felt passions about this phenomenon on the ground. The year 2020 alone has revealed how political crises force us to revisit old questions about identity and power.

Could we view power-sharing arrangements through the rearview window—of a 1980s Mercedes *service* or a TX4 hackney cab? In this thesis, I will try to do just that.

CHAPTER 2

SITES OF SOCIAL INTERACTION AND COHESION STRATEGIES: A THEORY OF ETHNIC TENSIONS AFTER POWER-SHARING AGREEMENTS

2.1: *Introduction*

What is the causal relationship between power-sharing arrangements and ethnic tensions in divided societies? How do institutions—designed to settle political violence—shape political behavior, and thus shape ethnic identity and antagonisms? Specifically, to what extent do power-sharing agreements increase or decrease ethnic tensions in post-conflict societies? This chapter lays the conceptual framework to tackle these research questions, adding to ethnic conflict and political violence literature. In short, the dual schemas of sites of social interaction (SSIs) and cohesion strategies explain how power-sharing affects ethnic tensions. Depending on specific SSIs and cohesion strategies, tensions may either increase or decrease. Taken as a whole, I establish a causal link between society (SSIs), institutional designs (cohesion strategies), ethnic tensions and the overall success or failure of a power-sharing regime. These theories contribute to the extensive body of literature in the sphere of ethnic conflict and conflict resolution, as evident in my literature review below.

2.2: *Literature Review*

As a political concept, power-sharing finds its roots in the seventeenth century, when German statesman Althusius coined the term "consociational" to "denote a polity consisting of an association of several societies."[24] The modern study of consociationalism, or sharing power among rival social and identity groups, is mostly attributed to Arend Lijphart's foundational investigation of the Netherlands' political system in the 1960s.[25] He situates "consociational democracy" in a typology of democratic systems.[26] It is no coincidence, however, that this concept gained traction during a global era of decolonization and wars of national liberation.[27] These conflicts, throughout the latter half of the twentieth century, made this subject especially relevant for social scientists and policymakers. Further interest grew in the 1990s—after the fall of the Soviet Union and the resulting ethnic conflicts in Eastern Europe—with the subfield integrating empirical innovations, like Ted Robert Gurr's *Minorities at Risk Project.*[28] With new social science methods and a fresh batch of relevant cases, consociational studies flourished.

Alongside the expansion of ethnic conflict studies was a parallel growth in conflict resolution studies. Here, many scholars turned their attention back to power-sharing theories of government by offering theoretical rebukes of Lijphart's and his contemporaries' schemas. Donald Horowitz counters Lijphart's consociational concepts of "inclusion, representation, and power sharing" with centripetalism, in which electoral institutions

---

[24] Rudy B. Andeweg, "Consociationalism," in *International Encyclopedia of the Social & Behavioral Sciences (Second Edition)*, ed. James D. Wright (Oxford: Elsevier, 2015), 692–94, https://doi.org/10.1016/B978-0-08-097086-8.93025-3, 692.

[25] Kristian Coates Ulrichsen, "Consociationalism," in *A Dictionary of Politics in the Middle East* (Oxford University Press, 2018), https://www.oxfordreference.com/view/10.1093/acref/9780191835278.001.0001/acref-9780191835278-e-85.

[26] Arend Lijphart, "Typologies of Democratic Systems," *Comparative Political Studies* 1, no. 1 (1969 1968): 3–44, 17-22.

[27] See Walker Connor, "Nation-Building or Nation-Destroying?," *World Politics* 24, no. 3 (1972): 319–55, https://doi.org/10.2307/2009753, and his engagement with Karl Deutsch, *Nationalism and Social Communication: An Inquiry into the Foundations of Nationality*, first published in 1953, 322-8.

[28] Ted Robert Gurr, "Peoples Against States: Ethnopolitical Conflict and the Changing World System: 1994 Presidential Address," *International Studies Quarterly* 38, no. 3 (1994): 347–77, https://doi.org/10.2307/2600737, 349.

incentivize cross-ethnic parties, "encouraging moderation."[29] Philip Roeder and Donald Rothchild, on the other hand, present "power dividing," in which institutions mirroring American political institutions—"civil liberties, multiple majorities, and checks and balances"—are emphasized.[30] This re-invigorated interest from academics and politicians in settling ethnic conflicts through power-sharing institutions has carried over into the twenty-first century.

To this end, scholars have identified a clear avenue for further investigation; that is, why power-sharing arrangements succeed or fail.[31] Principles espoused by earlier theorists have been explicitly integrated into peace settlements. For instance, proponents of power-sharing were instrumental in Iraq's new constitutional set-up after the 2003 war.[32] In the academic realm, Caroline Hartzell and Matthew Hoddie employ statistical analysis to study civil war conflict settlements and their outcomes from the 1970s to 1990s, finding durable peace in 87.5% of their cases.[33] Paulina Pospieszna and Gerald Schneider investigate how "war outcomes and the institutional legacy of conflict-affected countries" shape power-sharing

---

[29] See Matthijs Bogaards, "Consociationalism and Centripetalism: Friends or Foes?," *Swiss Political Science Review* 25, no. 4 (2019): 519–37, https://doi.org/10.1111/spsr.12371, 519. Bogaards provides a comprehensive overview of the two main opposing schools of consociational democracy in divided societies.

[30] Donald Rothchild and Philip Roeder, "Dilemmas of State-Building in Divided Societies," in Philip G. Roeder and Donald S. Rothchild, *Sustainable Peace: Power and Democracy after Civil Wars* (Ithaca: Cornell University Press, 2005), 15.

[31] Stefan Wolff, "Consociationalism, Power Sharing, and Politics at the Center," Oxford Research Encyclopedia of International Studies, March 1, 2010, https://doi.org/10.1093/acrefore/9780190846626.013.65, 19.

[32] See David L Phillips, "Power-Sharing in Iraq," *Council on Foreign Relations*, CRS No. 6, April, 2005, and Michael R. Gordon and Anthony Shadid, "U.S. Urges Iraqis to Try New Plan to Share Power," *The New York Times*, September 10, 2010, https://www.nytimes.com/2010/09/10/world/middleeast/10policy.html.

[33] Matthew Hoddie and Caroline Hartzell, "Civil War Settlements and the Implementation of Military Power-Sharing Arrangements," *Journal of Peace Research* 40, no. 3 (May 1, 2003): 303–20, https://doi.org/10.1177/0022343330304000300 4, 313.

institutions and political decision-making in divided societies.[34] Stephen Rosiny and Emer Groarke revive old debates about power-sharing's merits and limits around the ongoing Syrian civil war.[35] However, the burgeoning political science literature pertaining to ethnic conflict still lacks answers to fundamental questions and assumptions about power-sharing arrangements.

Nils-Christian Bormann et al. identify two specifically understudied areas in power-sharing theories: "[understanding] the causal chain from institutions to peace or conflict outcomes through behavior" and "the possibility that different kinds of power-sharing institutions may have different effects on civil peace."[36] Bormann and his colleagues conduct a large-N statistical analysis to test their hypotheses, finding that "de jure power-sharing institutions affect the likelihood of ethnic conflicts by influencing civil war *through* power-sharing practices [emphasis added]."[37] My research fleshes out Bormann et al.'s avenues for additional study and contributes to the overall subfield. There needs to be a comprehensive theory that accounts not only for the causal chain between power-sharing institutions and behaviors, but also how they influence ethnic animosities in post-conflict societies. Moreover, qualitative methods can better reveal specific factors that affect (and not affect) this causal chain. Instead of the statistical large-N approaches of Hartzell and Hoddie and Bormann et al., I plan to investigate this phenomenon through the comparative case study method, including within-case analysis and process-tracing, which is discussed later in this chapter. Only after teasing out these smaller questions do I plan to answer the big-picture question: Do power-sharing

---

[34] Paulina Pospieszna and Gerald Schneider, "The Illusion of 'Peace Through Power-Sharing': Constitutional Choice in the Shadow of Civil War," *Civil Wars* 15, no. sup1 (December 4, 2013): 44–70, https://doi.org/10.1080/13698249.2013.850877, 47.

[35] See Stephan Rosiny, "Power Sharing in Syria: Lessons from Lebanon's Taif Experience," *Middle East Policy* 20, no. 3 (2013): 41–55, https://doi.org/10.1111/mepo.12031; and Emer Groarke, "'Mission Impossible': Exploring the Viability of Power-Sharing as a Conflict-Resolution Tool in Syria," *International Journal of Conflict Management* 27, no. 1 (2016): 2–24, http://dx.doi.org/10.1108/IJCMA-12-2014-0090.

[36] Nils-Christian Bormann et al., "Power Sharing: Institutions, Behavior, and Peace," *American Journal of Political Science* 63, no. 1 (2019): 84–100, 86.

[37] Ibid., 96.

institutions work? But before I provide my theoretical framework, the next two sections define and operationalize seemingly amorphous terms like 'ethnicity' and 'tensions.'

2.3: *Defining Power-Sharing Agreements and Ethnic Tensions*

What are power-sharing agreements? What are ethnic tensions? While these questions seem relatively straightforward, these terms are up for debate because there is no consensus on their usages. Power-sharing is situated in the broader realm of consociationalism, which is concerned with regime type. John McGarry notes how consociation can be democratic or authoritarian.[38] There are a multitude of regime-type configurations, with much of the scholarly debate focused on which is the best institutional make-up for consociational democracy. Three main institutional frameworks emerge: power-sharing consociationalism, centripetalism, and power-dividing.[39] I adapt Stefan Wolff's categorizations to provide a simplified overview of each institutional design's recommendation, state construction, and status of rights and identities. This thesis will focus on power-sharing consociationalism, although these institutional frameworks are often combined in practice by nation-states.

---

[38] John McGarry, *The Northern Ireland Conflict: Consociational Engagements* (Oxford; New York: Oxford University Press, 2004), 1.

[39] See Arend Lijphart, *Democracy in Plural Societies: A Comparative Exploration* (New Haven: Yale University Press, 1977); Donald L. Horowitz, *Ethnic Groups in Conflict* (Berkeley: University of California Press, 1985); and Roeder and Rothchild, *Sustainable Peace.*

Figure 1. Three Main Institutional Designs for Power-Sharing[40]

Institutional Design	Power-Sharing Consociationalism	Centripetalism	Power-Dividing
Main Recommendation	Interethnic cooperation through coalition-building and joint executive decision-making	Interethnic cooperation through moderation induced by the electoral system	Pluralistic cooperation based on diverse interests and the separation of power
State Construction	Ethnic group-based political units	Interethnic political units	Interethnic political units
Status of Rights and Identities	Combination of group and individual rights	Individual rights	Individual rights
	Identity is public and private	Identity is private	Identity is private

Power-sharing agreements are settlements in which opposing factions, oftentimes in ethnic conflicts, agree to a formal set of political institutions that distributes power amongst each community. I will use power-sharing "agreements," "arrangements," and "institutions" to describe the same concept. Nevertheless, the contested nuance between each term should be acknowledged. For example, McGarry and his colleague Matt O'Leary emphasize the importance of an "…agreement on transitional issues that go beyond such [power-sharing] institutions" as part of their theory of liberal consociationalism.[41] The umbrella term "arrangements" can encompass a formalized treaty or agreement, or series of agreements and treaties which include the formation of power-sharing institutions. "Agreements" may

---

[40] Adapted from Wolff, "Consociationalism, Power Sharing, and Politics at the Center."
[41] McGarry, *The Northern Ireland Conflict*, 325.

imply a formal ratification process, which may not occur in all power-sharing regimes when informal pacts or precedents may take hold. As for "institutions," power-sharing must necessarily include some sort of constitutional prescription, in addition to state goals and issues of mutual concern that may not be embodied in de jure institutions. While Bosnia and Herzegovina formalized the Cabinet's distribution by ethnicity in their constitution, Lebanon's National Pact was originally an unwritten precedent that governed which religious group holds which office. These terms are interchangeable unless I note a clear differentiation.

Of course, power-sharing agreements are premised on the fact that there must be more than one political faction to share power with. The study of power-sharing in ethnic conflict assumes that political cleavages are formed in a polity through ethnicity. There are plenty of power-sharing arrangements without ethnicity as the defining cleavage in politics—one can look to the US Senate's February 2021 power-sharing agreement between Democrats and Republicans.[42] In this sense, power-sharing is a political tool: a means to achieve an end. This thesis explores the means-end link through the lens of ethnic conflict. In my study, political actors may represent their ethnic group as a whole or an ideological faction within an ethnic group. Power-sharing arrangements are reached between warring ethnic groups, often with the guarantee of an external state actor. Formal institutions within a power-sharing agreement include executive, legislative, and judiciary branches, as well as the mechanisms for the electoral process. With these considerations, power-sharing agreements may call for a new constitution, but it is not a necessary condition in all such agreements. Above all else, power-sharing aims to settle a violent ethnic conflict, and the hope for these agreements is that peace is achieved and stability is secured for a country and its people.

To better define ethnic tension, which often requires power-sharing, I will parcel out the words 'ethnic' and 'tension.' The idea of ethnicity is studied by scholars in multiple disciplines because of its salience and resonance in everyday life. In the United States, the 2020 Census

---

[42] Jack Brewster, "Senate Reaches Power-Sharing Agreement And Democrats Take Over Committees," *Forbes*, accessed March 25, 2021, https://www.forbes.com/sites/jackbrewster/2021/02/03/senate-reaches-power-sharing-agreement-and-democrats-take-over-committees/.

differentiates race and ethnicity when it pertains to an individual's "Hispanic origin."[43] Though this instance shows the practical uses of terms like "race" and "ethnicity" in a bureaucratic context, academics have defined ethnicity in different ways, depending on their focus.[44] In this examination, ethnicity is defined as a unit of social organization in which self-defined groups derive their commonality through a sense of common ancestry or lineage. This workable definition is in line with Anthony D. Smith's socialization theories, in which ethnicity is one manifestation of "the need for identification with a community in order to achieve individual identity and self-respect, [and] is in part a function of socialization experiences in the historic culture-community."[45] Section 2.4 will take a closer look at ethnicity, to underpin the conceptual logics of my framework of power-sharing and ethnic tensions.

Tension, used in conjunction with ethnicity, is described as antagonism, animosity or hatred between ethnic groups that manifests itself along a spectrum—in its extreme form as incidents of violence or in lesser degrees through prejudicial viewpoints and opinions of the out-group. I will use "tension" and "antagonism" interchangeably throughout this work. Ethnic tension is not ethnic conflict per se, but ethnic tension may precipitate incidents of violence and vice versa: violent conflict can de-escalate to a situation where there is peace, but tensions are still salient between formerly warring factions. Ethnic indifference, in which people may feel impartial or uninterested in a contest between ethnic identities, is not the same as ethnic tension. Implied is the fact that two or more ethnic groups must be present in the same contested territory. Although there are hierarchies and cleavages within an ethnic group (social class, region, gender, etc.), in my working definition, I focus on ethnic tensions between other ethnic groups. Also, tension assumes that the feelings are reciprocated by both groups. To reiterate, ethnic tension is animosity, antagonism and/or hatred

---

[43] US Census Bureau, "2020 Census Questions: Hispanic Origin," *2020Census.gov*, accessed November 10, 2020, https://2020census.gov/en/about-questions/hispanic-origin.html.

[44] See Clifford Geertz, "What Is a Country If It Is Not a Nation?," *The Brown Journal of World Affairs* 4, no. 2 (1997): 235–47.

[45] Anthony D. Smith, *The Ethnic Origins of Nations* (Oxford, UK : New York, NY, USA: BBlackwell, 1987), 14.

between identity groups, primarily derived from a generalizable ethnic characteristic.

2.4: *Understanding Ethnicity, Nationality, and the Nation-State*

What is ethnic conflict? What is the difference between ethnicity and nationality, or between state and nation? Fundamental to the key questions I pose is precisely defining these terms. "Nationality" is often conflated with "ethnicity," and while both ideas are heavily intertwined, each term must be separated from one another. Words like "state" and "nation" are used interchangeably in popular discourse, be it by journalists, politicians, and even the most astute scholars in academia.[46] As Walker Connor points out, "the most fundamental error involved in scholarly approaches to nationalism has been a tendency to equate nationalism with a feeling of loyalty to the state rather than with loyalty to the nation."[47] Ironically, this terminological obfuscation involves some of the most important terms in political science, not only in the academic realm but in the public sphere—especially when "…nation-ness is the most universally legitimate value in the political life of our time," as Benedict Anderson argues.[48] Before I embark on a theory of ethnicity, the first three terms I define and differentiate are 'state,' 'nation,' and 'nation-state.'

First, a state is the set of political institutions, collectively called

---

[46] See Clifford Geertz, "What Is a Country If It Is Not a Nation?," *The Brown Journal of World Affairs* 4, no. 2 (1997): 235–47, for a sociological account of the varying usages of each term; "Nations and States," accessed January 8, 2021, https://www.globalpolicy.org/component/content/article/172-general/30345-nations-and-states.html. This webpage gives an account of the popular understanding of the differences between 'nation' and 'state'; See "Remarks by President Trump to the 72nd Session of the United Nations General Assembly," *The White House*, accessed January 8, 2021, https://www.whitehouse.gov/briefings-statements/remarks-president-trump-72nd-session-united-nations-general-assembly/. Former president Trump describes the international delegation as "countries," "nations," and "nation-states" in one speech.
[47] Walker Connor, "Terminological Chaos ('A Nation Is a Nation, Is a State, Is an Ethnic Group, Is a …')," in *Ethnonationalism, The Quest for Understanding* (Princeton University Press, 1994), 89–117, https://doi.org/10.2307/j.ctv39x5s6.8, 91.
[48] Benedict R. Anderson, *Imagined Communities: Reflections on the Origin and Spread of Nationalism*, Rev. ed. (London; New York: Verso, 2006), 3.

"government," that is sovereign over people in a self-contained unit of territory. For my purposes, the Weberian definition of a state as an organization with the monopoly on legitimate violence should be recognized, but it is not the primary way I use this term.[49] The emphasis in this definition is that the state is contained within a territory, limited either by natural geographical demarcations or human-made borders. Central to this conceptualization is that the state is an entity that has ultimate power in decision-making in the polity, internally and externally. However, this does not necessarily mean this power is viewed as legitimate by all people in a state, which is partly the reason why internal conflict (like ethnic conflict) occurs. The state is manifested through government, a set of political institutions that control the levers of power in a society—and enforces its power through force or the threat of force. In international relations, states interact with other states, and has been the primary unit of analysis in this discipline. Mexico is a state, insofar as it has a government that exercises the final say and wields ultimate control over the levers of power (courts, police, immigration, monetary policy, education, etc.) within a delineated geographical unit.

Second, a nation is a self-defining, self-conscious group that derives its cohesion through a sense of common bond—real or perceived—as well as a sense of attachment to a physical space. People "sense" a nation precisely because the nation, as a unit, is self-perceived and intuitive.[50] It is not self-evident because "...the essence of a nation is intangible."[51] For example, in its common usage, many use the term in conjunction with a more tangible element of society, like "cultural nationalism" or "linguistic nationalism."[52] The nation is therefore rooted in feeling and intuition, as seen in the literature involving evolutionary psychology and group identities, like J.

---

[49] Andreas Anter, "The Modern State and Its Monopoly on Violence," *The Oxford Handbook of Max Weber*, March 5, 2020, https://doi.org/10.1093/oxfordhb/9780190679545.013.13.

[50] Andreas Wimmer, *Facing Ethnic Conflicts: Toward a New Realism* (Lanham, MD: Rowman & Littlefield Publishers, 2004), 24.

[51] Connor, "Terminological Chaos," 92.

[52] Ibid., 106.

Philippe Rushton's "Genetic Similarity Theory."[53] This fluidity, combined with Ernest Gellner's observation that "having a nation is not an inherent attribute of humanity, but it has now come to appear as such," makes it difficult to pinpoint the nation as a political phenomenon.[54] Nevertheless, the nation manifests itself in very real ways and has influenced the course of modern politics.

What makes the nation self-conscious is its self-defining nature, as the group and its individual members must be aware of their commonality to define what their nation is. This sentiment of belonging reinforces the very notion of a nation, which in turn, reinforces the self-defining capacity of group members to see themselves as forming a nation. Of course, one can counter that this is a characteristic of general identity formation, in individuals and groups. What differentiates a concept of nation, however, is how it perceives commonality with its group members. Many scholars associate "nation-ness" with "…a psychological dimension approximately that of the extended family, that is, a feeling of common blood lineage."[55] People form groupings around the basic family unit, then further extrapolate this sense of commonality by forming kinship groups that derive an intermediate common ancestry. Ultimately, these kinship bonds form an even greater bond that derives commonality through some perceived sense of shared ancestry, in the form of a nation. Civic nationalism, on the other hand, is forged through a commonality of ideas and shared values, or "the integration of citizens of by way of public discussion according to democratic procedures and the rule of law"

---

[53] J. Philippe Rushton, "Ethnic Nationalism, Evolutionary Psychology and Genetic Similarity Theory," *Nations and Nationalism* 11, no. 4 (2005): 489–507, https://doi.org/10.1111/j.1469-8129.2005.00216.x.

[54] Ernest Gellner, *Nations and Nationalism: New Perspectives on the Past* (Ithaca: Cornell University Press, 1983), 6.

[55] Connor, "Terminological Chaos," 94.

according to Donald Ipperciel.[56] In essence, the nation is in a constant process of self-defining, and this aspect of the nation has immense consequences on the role it plays in ethnic conflict.

A nation-state melds the tangible state and the intrinsically intangible nation, and nationalism is the ideological vehicle to achieve this. Simply put, the goal of national movements is to create their own nation-state. Nationalism is "...a theory of political legitimacy, which requires that ethnic boundaries should not cross political ones."[57] To clarify, nationalism involves a nation's self-defined territorial boundaries—a common homeland, or territory of origin. The nation, though intangible, lays claim to territory, by virtue of a common people being rooted in it. Eric Hobsbawm comments on the rise of nationalism in the nineteenth century, in which "rulers...rediscovered the importance of 'irrational' elements in the maintenance of the social fabric..." in the formation of nation-states.[58] The nation-state is elusive because there are no pure "nation-states." Many may consider Germany as a nation-state with a German national identity, yet the concept of a state for a so-called Germanic people arose during the wave of nineteenth-century European nationalist movements. Beforehand, this land was a collection of principalities under a broader confederation, be it the Holy Roman Empire or Napoleon's Confederation of the Rhine. Nation-states can seem like arbitrary concoctions, and only through the evolution—or re-definition—of one's nation can a nation-state be consolidated and claim legitimacy.

Ethnicity is related to nationality in the sense that ethnicity is also an identity which derives its manifestation through the self-defining, self-conscious grouping of people. A distinction though is that ethnicity

---

[56] Donald Ipperciel, "Constitutional Democracy and Civic Nationalism," *Nations and Nationalism* 13, no. 3 (2007): 395–416, https://doi.org/10.1111/j.1469-8129.2007.00293.x, 399-400; *Cf.* Yael Tamir, "Not So Civic: Is There a Difference Between Ethnic and Civic Nationalism?," *Annual Review of Political Science* 22, no. 1 (2019): 419–34, https://doi.org/10.1146/annurev-polisci-022018-024059. Tamir argues that in practice, the lines of ethnic and civic nationalism blur, so that no truly distinct civic nationalism can arise.

[57] Gellner, 1.

[58] Eric Hobsbawm, "Mass-Producing Traditions: Europe, 1870-1914," in *The Invention of Tradition* (Cambridge and New York, 1983), 263–307, 268.

derives its origins through a perceived blood relation. US citizens form the *American nation*, founded on civic nationalism. But except for those indigenous to the North American continent (Native Americans or First Nations), most cannot claim to be an *ethnic American*. Donald Horowitz asserts that ethnicity is ascriptive in nature, meaning that an ethnic grouping arises from qualities that are perceived to be beyond a person's control, "whether the indicium of group identity is color, appearance, language, religion, some other indicator of common origin, or some combination thereof."[59] The simple intuition that underlies ethnicity is that it is assumed to be immutable—that one is born into a certain ethnic group. As a way of sorting people into groups, conceptualizing ethnicity relies on culture and appearance, often reinforcing each other in its affirmation of distinctness in relation to others. Even religion, which until the Enlightenment was believed to be an inherited aspect of one's identity, still holds immense power in defining ethnic identity through the cultural practices and institutions that accompany religious practice—rather the actual belief in God. That is why in this study, though other scholars may make distinctions in ethnicity like "ethno-linguistic" or "ethno-religious," these are, in fact, ethnicities that revolve around a particular, prominent distinguishable cultural attribute.

In turn, ethnic conflict is the contestation of different ethnic groups over territory. It is a fight over "real estate."[60] Karl Cordell and Stefan Wolff aptly describe this phenomenon: "…at least one of the parties involved interprets the conflict, its causes and potential settlements along an existing or perceived discriminating ethnic divide…"[61] Ethnic conflicts are fights to assert hegemony over a disputed ethnic territory. A minority ethnic group may wish to gain hegemonic control while the majority ethnic group wishes to keep it. These expressions of power are sought to legitimize the societal standings of ethnic groups, as they seek either "to retain a measure

---

[59] Horowitz, 17-8.

[60] See James L. Gelvin, *The Israel-Palestine Conflict: One Hundred Years of War* (Cambridge University Press, 2014), https://doi.org/10.1017/CBO9781139583824, 3. Gelvin describes the Israel-Palestine conflict as "a dispute over real estate" and I find this quote applicable to most, if not all ethnic conflict.

[61] Karl Cordell, *Ethnic Conflict: Causes, Consequences, and Responses* (Cambridge ; Malden, MA: Polity, 2009), 83.

of political power it [an ethnic group] already possesses, or it strives to acquire the amount of power that it deems necessary in order to preserve its identity as a distinct ethnic group."[62] Certain groups resort to violent means when they perceive that the threat is so great to their community's preservation that nonviolent means cannot be pursued. A minority group may feel threatened by the majority ethnic group through a sense of injustice, discrimination, and/or relative deprivation. Intense mobilization, rooted in this insecurity, can result in what Barry Posen identifies as an ethnic security dilemma: "one group is likely to assume that another group's sense of identity, and the cohesion it produces, is a danger."[63] What distinguishes ethnic conflict from other forms of fighting is the total salience of ethnicity: "the permeative character of ethnic affiliations, by infusing so many sectors of social life, imparts a pervasive quality to ethnic conflict and raises sharply the stakes of ethnic politics."[64] Therefore, ethnic conflict is the battle over the legitimacy of an ethnic community to be sovereign over a disputed territory, and arises in divided societies when the threat of "ethnic elimination" is so great that only violent means will assure self-preservation and self-assertion.

2.5: *A Theoretical Framework for Ethnic Tensions after Power-Sharing Agreements*

As explored previously, the role of history and ancestry is integral to forming, consolidating, and crystallizing ethnic identities. Ethnic conflict takes the leap of faith, thrusting notions of ethnicity and nationality— these self-defining identities—into contestation. Peace settlements that involve power-sharing between ethnic groups politicizes ethnicity in formal institutions, but ideally ends ethnic violence as well. In this vein, an understanding of the conditions in which power-sharing may increase or decrease ethnic tensions in post-conflict societies can begin

---

[62] Ibid., 84.

[63] Barry R. Posen, "The Security Dilemma and Ethnic Conflict," *Survival* 35, no. 1 (March 1, 1993): 27–47, https://doi.org/10.1080/00396339308442672, 31; Daniel Byman, *Keeping the Peace: Lasting Solutions to Ethnic Conflicts* (Baltimore: Johns Hopkins University Press, 2002), 14-6.

[64] Horowitz, 7-8.

with a concept rooted in the study of historical memory: *lieux de mémoire*, roughly translated to "sites of memory." This historical schema will aid this exploration of post-conflict societies, if extrapolated to create a political science lens.[65]

Pierre Nora identifies and theorizes about a phenomenon that occurs after the advent of nineteenth-century nationalism. He calls it "sites of memory": "a play of memory and history, an interaction of two factors that result in their reciprocal overdetermination."[66] What concerns us in developing this theoretical framework is Nora's concept applied generally; that is, of sites or spheres where opposing forces are at play. These so-called *lieux*, taken literally or figuratively, are liminal places where divergent phenomena are forced to converge. Opposing concepts intermingle and interplay—either creating dissonance, tension, and antagonism or consonance, resolution, and even harmony—but nonetheless comprising one entity. This ontology is useful when adapted for the study political conflict and ethnic identity. Another characteristic of Nora's *lieux de mémoire* is the physical manifestation of this interplay between history and collective memory—in his case, through commemorative sites like cemeteries, monuments, and festivals.[67] The notion of "sites" that manifest themselves in real life is applicable for my analysis. These sites could be thought of as emanating throughout segments of society. It can be the various economic industries within a country; culture, humanities and the arts; education and sport; civil society groups and political institutions, and so on. Hence, the two fundamental characteristics in *lieux de mémoire*—a place of convergence of opposed entities and their manifestation in society, actual or perceived—put into perspective the way that opposing ethnic groups interact with one another in the same polity after peace is realized by means of power-sharing arrangements. These are what I call sites of social interaction (*lieux d'interaction sociale*, if you prefer).

---

[65] I must thank Professor Guy Beiner for exposing me to Pierre Nora's writings, when I took his course on historical commemoration in Ireland in the spring of 2020.
[66] Pierre Nora, "Between Memory and History: Les Lieux de Mémoire," *Representations*, no. 26 (1989): 7–24, https://doi.org/10.2307/2928520, 19.
[67] Ibid., 12.

Figure 2. A Typology of Sites of Social Interactions (SSIs) in Divided Societies

Type of SSI	Contestation	Coexistence	Collaboration
Expected Behavior	Fight Challenge Defend	Tolerance 'Stay-in-your-own-lane' mentality	Mutual benefit Intentional cross-community outreach
Identifying Characteristic(s)	Winners and losers Zero-sum game	Intermixing	Intermingling Shared spaces
Common Areas of Manifestation	Elections Political Institutions	Economy and Trade Transactional Relationships	Education Civil Society and NGOs
Example(s)	Belgian parliamentary politics (2010s)	Bosnian mixed villages (post-civil war)	South African Truth and Reconciliation Commission Indonesian *Kami Bangsa* education project

Taking into account the idea of sites of social interaction (or SSI for short), I devise a typological framework. Figure 2 shows three types of SSIs in post-conflict societies: sites of contestation, sites of coexistence, and sites of collaboration. In effect, these three categories encompass all facets of a country—be it the state, economy, or society. What differentiates this framework from other ways of categorizing a society is the way it places emphasis on examining the social fabric after prolonged violent conflict. Contestation most resembles the nature of society during civil war, while collaboration is expected in a society shared by ethnic groups. Coexistence is an in-between state, where ethnicity is salient but difference is tolerated. The benefit of conceptualizing post-conflict society as these types of sites, in a similar vein to Nora's illustration, is that it implies crossover potential in specific areas. Tension can only arise when opposing groups converge, whether in a larger territory or a local community. When viewing facets of political, social, and economic institutions through SSIs, one can determine the extent to which there is convergence or divergence within each site, and subsequently, measure the antagonism that may play out in a site. After all, ethnic identity needs a place to manifest itself, lay claim to group worth, and contrast or compare in relation to another group—and sites of contestation, coexistence, and collaboration are where these identities and any animosities play out in divided societies.

First, a site of contestation is a place where ethnic groups are expected to challenge and fight each other or defend from one another. They often involve substantial or essential issues to each group. In a site of contestation, there must be a winner and a loser—and thus, a zero-sum game may take hold.[68] For example, electoral systems are sites of contestation, where groups fight to win votes and secure the most advantage in government. Power-sharing agreements with strong corporatist elements are sure to create sites of contestation, not only in elections but in the state institutions themselves. The government, in a sense, is a site of contestation, but power-sharing institutions have mechanisms designed to moderate the winners and shelter the losers.[69] In practice, sites of contestation are places where identities may clash to the point of gridlock. Belgium's parliamentary politics is a good example of site of contestation: political parties divided on ethnic and linguistic lines continue to fail to form coalition governments in the recent decade, when "the big winners in the election could hardly

---

[68] Lijphart, *Democracy*, 27.

[69] For Lijphart's "consociational democracy," moderation is achieved via instruments of "mutual veto" and "segmental autonomy" while for Horowitz, power-sharing it is achieved through incentivizing cross-cutting coalitions in the electoral system.

be farther apart."[70] Overall, sites of contestation are characterized by a "winner-loser" playing field and is most common in politics in societies reeling from civil strife.

Second, a site of coexistence is a place where ethnic groups mix and show a level of tolerance—but nothing more. Ethnic identity is not a main concern. Rather, these sites tend to foster a "stay in your own lane" mentality. Opportunities for these sites may occur in the economy, if goods and services are rendered regardless of ethnic identification. In societies where ethnicity is the point of conflict, sites of coexistence can involve roads and public transportation, or other public spaces. Anders Stefansson's study of ethnic intermingling in mixed villages in Bosnia after their civil war concluded:

> "some level of inter-ethnic co-existence and tolerance had developed in particular between the returnees and displaced Serbs who had moved into these neighborhoods, among other things based on economic interdependence, an emerging sense of solidarity, and a pragmatic need to avoid conflict in everyday life."[71]

Arguments about sites of coexistence arise from its effectiveness; whether or not this form of "negative peace" is a constructive bridge towards greater trust-building or "merely hides the unresolved conflicts" in divided societies.[72] Pragmatic concerns like getting a job or leasing space for a business may override ethnic partisanship. These sites may shift depending on cultural contexts, but the primary indicator for a site of coexistence is an expectation for intermixing and tolerance.

Third, a site of collaboration is a place where ethnic groups are expected to intermingle, working together on common ground issues for mutual benefit. These sites are shared spaces, integrating intentional

---

[70] Suzanne Daley, "No Bridging Language Divide; Tensions Run Higher than Ever between Belgium's Two Halves," *National Post (Toronto)*, 2010.

[71] Anders H. Stefansson, "Coffee after Cleansing?: Co-Existence, Co-Operation, and Communication in Post-Conflict Bosnia and Herzegovina," *Focaal* 2010, no. 57 (2010): 62–76, https://doi.org/10.3167/fcl.2010.570105, 7.

[72] Ibid., 11.

cross-community efforts and resulting in mutually beneficial outcomes for all ethnic groups involved. Power-sharing arrangements may have provisions for sites of collaboration. For instance, efforts to foster reconciliation, dialogue, and cross-cultural exchanges promote understanding of opposing ethnic groups. South Africa's "Truth and Reconciliation" commission was premised on the fact that restorative justice could be achieved by having victims and perpetrators of ethnic violence attest to the tragedies of apartheid, as a process of healing.[73] Sites of collaboration can arise organically or constructed by political agreement. Civic groups and NGOs in many countries view education as a way to bridge community animosities, especially at the primary and secondary school level. The *Kami Bangsa Indonesia* project, for example, seeks to foster "engaged citizenship" and "tolerance" among students in "six Indonesia provinces widely regarded as conflict areas, post-conflict areas, or areas of concern.[74] In these sites, there are elements of mutual benefit concerned with ethnic communities, but overall, sites of collaboration are meant to be shared spaces in which a sense of community can be forged from the aftermath of war.

Power-sharing arrangements pursue strategies, to reach an overarching objective: creating a functionally cohesive, stable polity after internal, interethnic conflict. Of course, other objectives, like distributing the spoils of war, are pursued by the opposing parties. But in the end, power-sharing agreements are a means to an end: reconstituting a country. Adopting a strategic level approach to power-sharing institutions enhances the previous discussion on social interaction, revealing a clearer picture of the casual relationship between power-sharing and ethnic tensions. Strategy accounts for particular power-sharing institutional designs, and how specific designs may affect ethnic tensions. I use this dual-pronged approach, in tackling this question, to amplify my theory's explanatory power. The three types of cohesion strategies are: assimilation, differentiation, and segregation. Figure 3 summarizes each strategy and its characteristics.

---

[73] See Timothy Sisk and Christoph Stefes, "Power Sharing as an Interim Step in Peace Building: Lessons from South Africa" in Roeder and Rothchild, *Sustainable Peace.*

[74] "External Evaluation - Indonesia," *Center for Civic Education*, accessed January 8, 2021, https://www.civiced.org/civitas/program/research-and-evaluation/indonesia.

Figure 3. A Typology of Cohesion Strategies in Divided Societies

Cohesion Strategies	Assimilation	Differentiation	Segregation
Intention	Absorb ethnic groups into a dominant or overarching identity	Maintain and acknowledge differences between ethnic groups	Separate ethnic groups within the polity
Outcome	Hegemonic ethnic identity, adopted as national identity Novel national identity	Pluralistic national identity Multicultural national identity	Bifurcation of national identity
Historical Example(s)	Post-Franco Spain language policy Post-apartheid South Africa	Malaysian economic development	Baghdad neighborhoods (post-2003 Iraq War) Bangsamoro (Philippines)

Assimilation is a strategy intended to absorb the 'other' into the dominant identity or a new, national identity. Two outcomes are possible: either a dominant ethnic group integrates minority groups into their own, making the dominant ethnic identity the hegemonic national identity, or a new, overarching national identity is constructed and all other ethnicities are subsumed under this newly-formed identity 'umbrella.' Avidit Archarya et al. explore assimilation in ethnically divided societies through a "sons-of-the-soil" model, in which a national elite is faced with a set of choices: "(i) whether or not to exert effort toward population control, and (ii) whether or not to exert effort in assimilating the population of the other group."[75]

---

[75] Avidit Acharya, David D. Laitin, and Anna Zhang, "'Sons of the Soil': A Model of Assimilation and Population Control," *Journal of Theoretical Politics* 30, no. 2 (2018): 184–223, https://doi.org/10.1177/0951629817737858, 186.

These choices are made both during negotiations for power-sharing and after a settlement is reached through the implementation process.

As a rule of thumb, the bigger the difference among ethnic groups, the harder it is to pursue a successful assimilation strategy. In post-Franco Spain, an assimilation policy that imposed the Spanish language in education and administrative positions had "low cost" barriers for Catalonians because Castilian and Catalan languages are structurally similar.[76] However, assimilation can be a very costly endeavor. Many decry such moves as 'cultural genocide.' A recent example is the ongoing efforts of the Chinese government to assimilate the Uighur minority in Xinjiang province through 're-education camps' and mass-surveillance. This is evidence, as many claim, that "China is committing crimes against humanity in its treatment of the Uighurs."[77] China's forced assimilation policy is one end of the extreme but is not a unique phenomenon. Assimilation, be it under the dominant ethnic culture or a new national culture (e.g. "South African" after apartheid) are seen in divided societies after violent conflict. Through successful assimilation, cohesion is achieved at the state level—either voluntarily or forcibly. Unsuccessful assimilation, however, may result in the re-emergence of conflict.

Differentiation, or a strategy in which ethnic diversity is accepted, is rooted in a pluralistic notion of society. The term "differentiation" is used, instead of "diversity," because it encompasses the relational nature of ethnicity in divided societies. Rather than something valued in its own right, as diversity has come to signify in present-day parlance, differentiation has a more neutral connotation.[78] This concept is embedded in the idea of power-sharing, as "even if political mobilization is organized on ethnic lines, civil politics can be maintained if ethnic elites adhere to a

---

[76] Ibid., 196-7.

[77] Kate Cronin-Furman, "China Has Chosen Cultural Genocide in Xinjiang—For Now," *Foreign Policy*, accessed January 10, 2021, https://foreignpolicy.com/2018/09/19/china-has-chosen-cultural-genocide-in-xinjiang-for-now/.

[78] See "How Diversity Makes Us Smarter," *Greater Good*, accessed March 26, 2021, https://greatergood.berkeley.edu/article/item/how_diversity_makes_us_smarter. Corporate America is a prime example of a societal push for greater diversity. I wanted to use the term 'differentiation' instead so that the political baggage that may come with the rhetoric of diversity is avoided.

power-sharing bargain that equitably protects all groups."[79] Two outcomes of differentiation strategy develop: cultural pluralism and multiculturalism. Cultural pluralism, a principle in which *"cultural differences* would be acknowledged and respected" so that it "[enriches] a vital democracy," contrasts from multiculturalism, a principle that emphasizes cultural differences and espouses cultural relativism.[80] Lloyd Wong's sociological paradigm corresponds to the outcomes of differentiation I propose—cultural pluralism parallels "interactive pluralism" while multiculturalism parallels "fragmented pluralism" in society.[81]

Differentiation is a strategy that many post-conflict societies adhere to, especially if they have democratic power-sharing institutions. For instance, Abdul Rahman Embong examines Malaysian society's transition to a differentiated middle class: "unlike the pre-1970s period, when the new middle class in Malaysia was overwhelmingly Chinese, the contemporary new Malaysian middle class is multiethnic in composition, with the new Malay middle class constituting a major component."[82] Tolerance is emphasized in a strategy of differentiation, so that members of oppositional ethnic groups may interact with each other in spheres where ethnicity is not as salient, like in trade or commerce. While cultural pluralism prefers respect for differences, multiculturalism takes one step further, emphasizing differences (and to detractors, exasperating them). In this vein, cultural pluralism and multiculturalism are the same side of the coin but differ in the extent to which differentiation is desired in society.

The third outcome of divided societies is segregation, either

---

[79] Chaim Kaufmann, "Possible and Impossible Solutions to Ethnic Civil Wars," *International Security* 20, no. 4 (1996): 136–75, 6.

[80] Richard J. Bernstein, "Cultural Pluralism," *Philosophy & Social Criticism* 41, no. 4–5 (May 1, 2015): 347–56, https://doi.org/10.1177/0191453714564855, 350; Lloyd Wong, "Multiculturalism and Ethnic Pluralism in Sociology," in *Revisiting Multiculturalism in Canada: Theories, Policies and Debates*, ed. Shibao Guo and Lloyd Wong (Rotterdam: SensePublishers, 2015), 69–90, https://doi.org/10.1007/978-94-6300-208-0_5, 71-3.

[81] Wong, 72.

[82] Abdul Rahman Embong, "The Culture and Practice of Pluralism in Postcolonial Malaysia," in Robert W. Hefner, ed., *The Politics of Multiculturalism: Pluralism and Citizenship in Malaysia, Singapore, and Indonesia* (University of Hawai'i Press, 2001), 59–85, https://www.jstor.org/stable/j.ctt6wqpj7.5, 61-2.

self-imposed by groups or rendered through government policies and international treaties. In ethnic conflict, segregation via migration occurs in mixed ethnicity neighborhoods. This tendency towards homogeneity during ethnic violence is because "attacks are more likely to occur in areas where there are small but significant minorities."[83] Nils Wiedmann and Idean Salehyan's study of the steady self-segregation of Sunni and Shia neighborhoods in Baghdad during the 2003 Iraq War convincingly proves this phenomenon.[84] Living areas are gradually homogenized because as people became easy targets of ethnic violence in mixed areas, they moved to find safety amongst their own ethnic group. This is proven to reduce ethnic violence in the long run—and scholars like Chaim Kaufmann propose this type of "ethnic separation" as a solution to ethnic civil wars.[85]

The dilemma after peace is achieved, however, is whether or not communities should stay segregated. In this case, a strategy of segregation may be pursued through power-sharing agreements—explicitly or implicitly—to maintain peace. In its hardest form of segregation, opposing ethnic groups only come into contact with each other in sites of contestation. This results in a bifurcation of national identity, allowing room for minority national sentiments to be expressed in political institutions. Ethnicities geographically isolated in a territory may benefit from a strategy of segregation, allowing for autonomous political institutions from the centralized government. Marshaley J. Baquiano analyzes the psychological positioning between the Philippine government and the Moro Islamic Liberation Front (MILF), an insurgency group fighting for an independent state in southern Philippines. Due to the isolation of the minority ethnic-religious Muslims relative to the rest of the country, the insurgency group lays claim to the "Bangsamoro people" and "state."[86] Both parties pursued a segregation strategy, allowing the ethnic Moros to have autonomous

---

[83] Nils B. Weidmann and Idean Salehyan, "Violence and Ethnic Segregation: A Computational Model Applied to Baghdad," *International Studies Quarterly* 57, no. 1 (March 1, 2013): 52–64, https://doi.org/10.1111/isqu.12059, 60.

[84] See Weidmann and Salehyan.

[85] Kaufmann, "Possible," 7.

[86] See Marshaley J. Baquiano, "Intergroup Positioning in Peace Negotiations: The Bangsamoro Peace Talks in the Philippines," *Peace and Conflict: Journal of Peace Psychology* 25, no. 3 (August 2019): 234–45, http://dx.doi.org/10.1037/pac0000360.

political institutions in the Philippines. In this case, separating the ethnic minority from national politics has helped achieve peace.

2.6: *Do Power-Sharing Agreements Increase or Decrease Ethnic Tensions?*

Power-sharing agreements reflect the will of elite combatants in ethnic conflict to resort to the negotiating table when there seems to be no incentive to prolonged violence in the short-term or when an external actor with overwhelming force intervenes, either in favor of one side or as a 'neutral' arbitrator. During negotiations, elites propose power structures that benefit their ethnic communities. Political institutions, governance, and the electoral process are essential spheres for negotiation. Compared to other forms of conflict settlement, power-sharing "refers to a practice of conflict settlement that has a form of self-government regime at heart, but whose overall institutional design includes a range of further mechanisms for the accommodation of ethnic diversity in divided societies."[87] Most power-sharing agreements favor corporatist structures, in which power is segmented into main interest groups—that being the main ethnic communities in conflict. This differs from a pluralistic political structure, which accounts for different interests and beliefs on the individual level. External powers often act as guarantors for power-sharing agreement and help in the maintenance of peace in the short term.[88] The corporatist, elite-centric agreements achieve peace in the short run, but "…create incentives for ethnic leaders to escalate both the stakes and the means of conflict."[89] This means that political elites are incentivized to keep ethnic divisions salient. But do these divisions influence ethnic tensions in the long run, after peace is achieved?

In short, power-sharing institutions *do* influence ethnic tensions, and depending on certain conditions, may increase or decrease tensions in post-conflict societies in the long run. The normative effect of these institutions should not be underestimated. Constructivist arguments may

---

[87] Wolff, "Consociationalism, Power Sharing, and Politics at the Center," 17.

[88] See Marie Joëlle Zahar, "Power Sharing in Lebanon: Foreign Protectors, Domestic Peace, and Democratic Failure" in Roeder and Rothchild, *Sustainable Peace.*

[89] Philip Roeder, "Power Dividing as an Alternative to Ethnic Power Sharing," in Roeder and Rothchild, *Sustainable Peace,* 56.

gain credibility as power-sharing regimes play out decades after their settlement. A key differentiator of these agreements are those concerning solely the state's political institutions and those that account for cross-community social interaction outside the realm of politics. Even if cross-community provisions are outlined in original settlements, the recent histories of divided societies after conflict should attest as to whether or not these efforts were implemented. Under what conditions do power-sharing agreements increase or decrease ethnic tensions in a divided country?

Figure 4. Relationship Between Theoretical Frameworks and Ethnic Tension in Post-Conflict Societies

Theory	SSIs			Cohesion Strategies		
Type	Contestation	Coexistence	Collaboration	Assimilation	Differentiation	Segregation
Ethnic Tension	Increase	Increase/ Decrease	Decrease	Increase	Increase/ Decrease	Decrease
Power-Sharing Predicted Outcome	Failure	Limited Failure/ Limited Success	Success	Failure	Limited Failure/ Limited Success	Success

Using the sites of social interactions laid out in Figure 2 coupled with the cohesion strategies of divided societies after power-sharing agreements laid out in Figure 3, I generate three causal hypotheses about the relationship between power-sharing and ethnic tensions. First, in post-conflict societies, sites of contestation increase ethnic tensions, while sites of collaboration decrease ethnic tensions. Sites of coexistence may either increase or decrease animosities, depending on case-specific factors (H1). Second, in power-sharing arrangements, a cohesion strategy of assimilation will increase ethnic tensions, while a cohesion strategy of segregation will decrease ethnic tensions. A cohesion strategy of differentiation will either increase or decrease ethnic tensions, contingent on the sites of contestation, coexistence, and collaboration contained in a power-sharing agreement (H2). Power-sharing agreements that institutionalize and implement SSIs and cohesion strategies that, on balance, increases ethnic tensions will fail, while power-sharing agreements that institutionalize and implement SSIs and cohesion strategies conducive to a decrease in ethnic tensions will succeed (H3). Figure 4 outlines each theory's relationship with ethnic tensions in a divided society with power-sharing institutions.

H1: In post-conflict societies, sites of contestation increase ethnic tensions, while sites of collaboration decrease ethnic tensions. Sites of coexistence may either increase or decrease tensions, depending on case-specific factors.

Hypothetically, at its most extreme, society in the midst of civil war is altogether a site of contestation. In this scenario, war is a zero-sum game involving the self-preservation of ethnic collectivities. Many power-sharing agreements are struck in the context of a peace settlement, because warring factions desire to guarantee their political position in a reconstituted state. Whereas sites of contestation are spheres in which ethnic tensions are high because groups view these places as a zero-sum game, sites of collaboration have low ethnic tension because these areas are viewed as a shared space. Sites of coexistence fall in between, where tensions might be salient, but tolerance of others is expected. Tensions may remain in sites of coexistence but are not salient to the extent of sites of contestation.

H2: In power-sharing arrangements, a cohesion strategy of assimilation will increase ethnic tensions, while a cohesion strategy of segregation will decrease ethnic tensions. A cohesion strategy of differentiation will either increase or decrease ethnic tensions, depending on the sites of contestation, coexistence, and collaboration contained in a power-sharing agreement.

I also argue in Figure 4 that power-sharing that pursues an assimilation strategy increases ethnic tensions, while policies of segregation decrease tensions. Oftentimes, assimilation will increase ethnic tensions but if a hegemonic culture (either of one ethnic group or a new culture) is forced upon other groups successfully, this tension may be buried and overcome by government. A failed policy of assimilation will exacerbate ethnic tensions to the point of renewed conflict. On the other hand, the segregation of ethnic groups will decrease ethnic tensions in the long run due to the homogeneity. This, hypothetically, would eliminate ethnic tensions between different groups altogether because they do not come into contact with each other. This view is in line with Kaufmann's solution to ethnic conflict, as he claims, "separation may help reduce inter-ethnic antagonism; once real security threats are reduced, the plausibility of hypernationalist appeals may eventually decline."[90] But in diverse, mixed societies this goal incurs heavy costs in the short run. These two extreme goals that certain power-sharing agreements have also carry extreme outcomes in regard to increasing or decreasing ethnic animosities.

Moreover, I propose that a power-sharing strategy of differentiation may increase or decrease tension, depending on the extent to which there are sites of contestation, coexistence, and/or collaboration in a divided society. Differentiation may result in less tension because sites of coexistence and collaboration are created, either 'top-down' from government policies and power-sharing agreements or 'bottom-up' from a potential cross-community civil society. But this is very hard to do. One route that Hugo Miall proposes is "conflict transformation," which calls for "a process of engaging with and transforming the relationships, the interests, the discourses, and, if necessary, the very constitution of society that supports the continuation of violent conflict."[91] Such transformation would be needed to successfully implement a policy of ethnic pluralism that decreases ethnic tensions. Certain conditions, in contrast, may cause animosity to increase in a strategy of differentiation—and sites of social interaction are key to determining whether tensions increase or decrease. Accordingly, a policy of differentiation may be a mixed bag for ethnic relations in a divided society.

H3: Power-sharing agreements that institutionalize and implement SSIs and cohesion strategies that on balance increases ethnic tensions will fail, while power-sharing agreements that institutionalize and implement SSIs

---

[90] Kaufmann, "Possible," 11.

[91] Hugo Miall, "Transforming Ethnic Conflict: Theories and Practices" in Wimmer, *Facing Ethnic Conflicts*, 162.

and cohesion strategies conducive to a decrease in ethnic tensions will succeed.

Granted that power-sharing arrangements incorporate sites of social interaction and cohesion strategies in their frameworks, both typologies and their causal links to ethnic tensions can predict the success or failure of a power-sharing regime in the long run. The main determinant for power-sharing success or failure is a regime's stability, both politically and socially. Power-sharing arrangements that provide for stable governance in the long run—including a functioning bureaucracy, free and fair elections, and the rule of law—are successful. Failed power-sharing regimes are characterized by state dysfunction, and in its most extreme, power-sharing collapse or civil war. I posit that increased ethnic tensions in a polity increases the likelihood for power-sharing failure. Likewise, I expect decreased ethnic tensions increases the chances for success. Ethnic tensions, if unchecked, spiral into incidents of violence and renewed ethnic grievances—the precursor for conflict. That is why higher increases necessarily increases the likelihood of regime failure. Conversely, if tensions are checked and decreased, this decreases the likelihood of failure. In short, there is an inverse relationship between ethnic tensions and power-sharing outcomes. Hypothesis 3 incorporates both causal frameworks in an attempt to answer fundamental questions about the desirability of power-sharing institutions as a conflict resolution mechanism, especially in the long run. This links power-sharing arrangements' effects on ethnic tensions in society to the viability of a power-sharing state.

Figure 5. How Power-Sharing affects Ethnic Tensions in Post-Conflict Societies

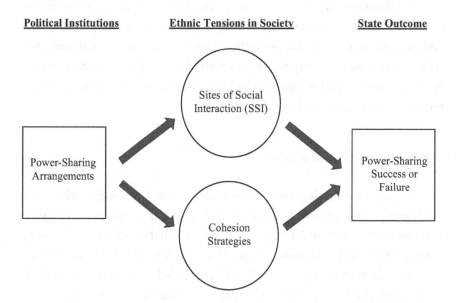

Figure 5 demonstrates the causal chains that unite all three hypotheses, to form a comprehensive theory of how power-sharing agreements affect ethnic tensions in post-conflict societies. Inherent in these arguments is the assumption that ethnic conflict is not purely rational nor irrational— rather, it is a mix of power and identity. The claims I provide lean towards a constructivist view of group identity and ultimately, the normative aspect of power-sharing institutions. Though certain scholars like Michael Hechter view that "ethnonationalism can be *collectively* irrational, for it is often associated with undesirable social outcomes like economic decline and civil war," others like Barry Posen argue that ethnic conflict results from security dilemmas among mobilized armed communities in a state of "internal anarchy.[92] Power-sharing agreements can thus provide political and 'rational' solutions to violent conflicts, but may not address core issues of identity and nationalism. What I conclude, through a theoretical

---

[92] Michael Hechter, "Containing Ethnonationalist Violence," in Wimmer, 284-5; See Chaim Kaufmann, "Rational Choice and Progress in the Study of Ethnic Conflict: A Review Essay," *Security Studies* 14, no. 1 (2005): 178–207, https://doi.org/10.1080/09636410591002554, 199.

framework of ethnic tensions and power-sharing arrangements after peace is achieved, closely aligns to Rothchild and Roeder's conclusions: "The very same institutions that provide an attractive basis to end a conflict in an ethnically divided country are likely to hinder the consolidation of peace and democracy over the longer term."[93] By studying ethnic tensions and their correspondence to types of power-sharing agreements, one can test if power-sharing is an adequate vehicle for long-term peace or just a short-term stopgap to curb violent ethnic conflict.

2.7: *Research Method and Design*

As discussed earlier, this thesis will rely on the comparative case study method rather than large or small-*N* statistical analysis. I will study Lebanon and Northern Ireland, two countries that experienced civil war among rival ethnic-religious groups. Both cases resolved ethnic conflict via power-sharing arrangements: 1989 Taif Accords for Lebanon and 1998 Belfast Agreement for Northern Ireland. It has been over thirty years since the Taif Accords and over twenty years since the Good Friday Agreement, so there has been ample time since power-sharing was struck in both nations to assess their impact. The main variation between Lebanon and Northern Ireland is Lebanon's relative state failure and Northern Ireland's state success. Both cases involve power-sharing, however Lebanon's power-sharing institutions have utterly collapsed while Northern Ireland's institutions have mostly held in place. With this in mind, I design a "structured, focused comparison," using "controlled comparison" as described by Alexander George and Andrew Bennett's case method.[94]

Each case study will involve a textual analysis of the power-sharing treaties and smaller studies on certain facets provisioned in each agreement. First, I will conduct a brief historical background of the ethnic conflict in each society. Then, I will analyze the legal text of the two power-sharing agreements—the Taif and Good Friday agreements—and conclude with

---

[93] Donald Rothchild and Philip Roeder, "Dilemmas of State-Building in Divided Societies," in Roeder and Rothchild, *Sustainable Peace*, 6.

[94] See Chapters 3 and 8 in Alexander L. George, *Case Studies and Theory Development in the Social Sciences*, BCSIA Studies in International Security (Cambridge, Mass.: MIT Press, 2005).

the extent to which these plans were implemented and/or altered over the course of their ratification to the present-day. To better understand the sites of social interactions and cohesion strategy theories, I will select key provisions in the documents and determine which site and strategy is purported to be achieved. Using statistical data, studies, and public opinion via polling and news outlets, I determine if these sites of social interaction and cohesion strategies correspond to the extent of ethnic tension in the country, as I predict. In summary, this theoretical framework will be tested through two case studies to see if power-sharing does increase or decrease ethnic tension and if the factors addressed above contribute to such changes.

2.8: *Conclusion*

Milton J. Esman notes that "human behavior is conditioned decisively by opportunities and constraints provided by the institutions that people encounter."[95] This chapter builds a theoretical argument that power-sharing agreements have the potential to both increase or decrease ethnic tensions in divided societies after peace, depending on an agreement's cohesion strategy and provisions for sites of social interaction. Incorporating the rich body of research on ethnic conflict, I conceptualize abstract notions of 'nation' and 'ethnicity,' and clearly defined what power-sharing agreements and ethnic tensions are. Then, I present two analytical frameworks to help us in this investigation: sites of social interaction, necessary for animosity to arise in a divided society and cohesion strategies, central to the goal of power-sharing institutions. I devised this two-pronged approach to better examine causality between societal behaviors, institutional designs, and ethnic tensions. Together, this approach yields the conclusion that sites of contestation increase ethnic tensions, sites of collaboration decrease tensions, and sites of coexistence may increase or decrease tensions contingent on specific case factors. The cohesion strategy of assimilation will increase ethnic animosities while segregation will decrease them— differentiation, in the middle-ground, can either increase or decrease

---

[95] Milton J. Esman, "Ethnic Pluralism: Strategies for Conflict Management," in Wimmer, *Facing Ethnic Conflicts*, 203.

tension depending on the extent to which sites of social interaction are cultivated by power-sharing.

Sites of social interaction and cohesion strategies give a comprehensive view of the group behavior and institutional mechanisms in post-conflict societies. Granted that both schemas hold up to my subsequent empirical studies, I predict that ethnic tension is one determining factor in power-sharing regime outcomes, in the long run. My last hypothesis posits that in the long-term perspective, an overall increase in a society's ethnic tensions will cause power-sharing failure, while a decrease will cause power-sharing success. Like my other theories, power-sharing may result in limited success or failure if, on the balance, ethnic tensions have only slightly increased or decreased. In conclusion, power-sharing agreements have a normative impact on divided societies and studying the ethnic tensions (or lack thereof) after their implementation can reveal new ways to determine if power-sharing succeeds or fails in varying post-conflict societies around the world.

CHAPTER 3

LEBANON: A NATION FACES A TOUGH REALITY

"It is a Syrian solution in an Arab dress beneath an international umbrella."

– Adel Malek, political analyst, on the Taif Accords, 1989.[96]

"I think Beirut now is not the same as it was before I became prime minister. Now, everybody admits that Beirut now, and Lebanon in general, and Beirut in particular, is coming back to being the jewel of the Middle East."

– Lebanese prime minister Rafik Hariri, in an interview with reporter Charlie Rose, 1998.[97]

"Our response to this decision is that whoever declares or starts a war, be it brother or father, then it is our fight to defend ourselves and our existence."

– Hassan Nasrallah, leader of Hezbollah, after the paramilitary group took over the streets of Beirut, 2008.[98]

3.1: *Introduction*

The Preamble of the Lebanese Constitution states: "The abolition of political confessionalism shall be a basic national goal and shall be achieved

---

[96] Youssef M. Ibrahim, "LEBANESE FACTIONS AGREE ON CHARTER TO RESOLVE STRIFE," *The New York Times*, October 23, 1989, https://www.nytimes.com/1989/10/23/world/lebanese-factions-agree-on-charter-to-resolve-strife.html.

[97] *Rafic Hariri - Charlie Rose*, accessed March 21, 2021, https://charlierose.com/videos/13778.

[98] Nada Bakri and Graham Bowley, "Confrontation in Lebanon Appears to Escalate," *The New York Times*, May 8, 2008, https://www.nytimes.com/2008/05/08/world/middleeast/09lebanon.html.

according to a staged plan."[99] Three decades later, this "staged plan" does not exist for a country roughly the size of Connecticut—even after a fifteen-year civil war claimed 150,000 lives, 300,000 casualties, and over 1 million émigrés.[100] As of March 2021, the Lebanese political system is in limbo after the resignation *en masse* of prime minister Hassan Diab's government in August 2020, because, as *The Daily Star* puts it, "political factions waste time over sectarian considerations in Cabinet formation."[101] Some analysts argue that Lebanon is a failed state, considering these staggering numbers in 2020: 75% of its people live in poverty, the country's public debt is 175% of its GDP, and there are 1.7 million refugees, making Lebanon the state with the highest per capita refugee population in the world.[102] However, most do agree on what has caused the country's recent social and economic spiral—political corruption, wrought by "[Lebanon's] dysfunctional sectarian political system."[103] Why have Lebanon's political institutions stagnated, thirty years later? The answer may lie in power-sharing and ethnic tensions after the dust settled from the civil war.

This chapter explores Lebanon's power-sharing constitution to determine the extent to which ethnic tensions have increased or decreased since the 1989 Taif Accords. I trace a history of power-sharing in the region, dating back to the Ottoman era. This legacy culminated in the creation of *Grand Liban* during the French Mandate, institutionalizing

---

[99] See The Preamble, Section 8, "The Lebanese Constitution," *Arab Law Quarterly* 12, no. 2 (1997): 224–61, 225.

[100] *Lebanon's Civil War: Seven Lessons Forty Years On,* European Union Institute for Security Studies, (LU: Publications Office, 2015), https://data.europa.eu/doi/10.2815/475463, 1 and "Lebanon vs. Connecticut (USA): Comparea Area Comparison," accessed January 4, 2021, http://www.comparea.org/LBN+US_CT.

[101] "Hariri, Aoun Discuss Govt after Hiatus," *The Daily Star - Lebanon*, December 7, 2020, Access World News, https://infoweb.newsbank.com/apps/news/document-view?p=AWNB&docref=news/17F9CC497E5D7F8.

[102] "Is Lebanon a Failed State? Here's What the Numbers Say," *Council on Foreign Relations*, accessed January 4, 2021, https://www.cfr.org/in-brief/lebanon-failed-state-heres-what-numbers-say.

[103] Mohamad Bazzi, "The Corrupt Political Class That Broke Lebanon," *Foreign Affairs*, December 8, 2020, https://www.foreignaffairs.com/articles/lebanon/2020-08-14/corrupt-political-class-broke-lebanon; See Steven A. Cook, "Lebanon as We Know It Is Dying," *Foreign Policy*, accessed January 4, 2021, https://foreignpolicy.com/2020/07/30/lebanon-as-we-know-it-is-dying/.

a consociational society. Due to various socio-economic developments, however, the political arrangement that favored Maronite Catholics was unsustainable, which led to the Lebanese civil war in 1975. I proceed to identify the cohesion strategies and sites of social interaction in Taif. In its totality, I extrapolate underlying SSIs of coexistence and cohesion strategies of assimilation and differentiation. Although the power-sharing agreement contained contradictory strategic goals, it does envision a broad, national identity based on the common denominator between the religious sects: the Arab identity.

Then, I assess Lebanese society, and how it has adapted to a post-conflict reality through its sites of contestation, coexistence, and collaboration. In education, a site of collaboration pursuing assimilation through a national Arab identity is envisioned in Taif. In the economic reconstruction and displacement policies of the new government, sites of coexistence and collaboration were conceived. Unfortunately, a history of both cases demonstrates that these provisions in the Taif Accords were barely implemented. Education and the economy became sites of contestation, which led to a corresponding increase in ethnic tensions. This conclusion is upheld through my study of ethnic tensions since peace was achieved in Lebanon. Lastly, I conclude with my findings of the role that Taif played in cultivating—or failing to cultivate—sites of social interaction conducive to decreasing ethnic tensions. There is a causal link between cohesion strategies and sites of social interaction and a rise in ethnic tension in Lebanon. This unique theoretical perspective on Lebanon's power-sharing institutions provides one of many causal factors that contributed to the country's current dilapidated state—a far cry from the "extraordinary opportunity" embodied in the Taif Accords.[104]

3.2: *An Enduring History of Power-Sharing in Lebanon*

The people of the area known as Lebanon have coexisted in a mosaic of different religious sects for centuries prior to the creation of the modern

---

[104] Thomas L. Friedman, "U.S. Hails Lebanon Accord and Urges Support," *The New York Times*, October 24, 1989, https://www.nytimes.com/1989/10/24/world/us-hails-lebanon-accord-and-urges-support.html.

nation-state in the 1920s. This milieu of communities trace their origins to the period of Islamic rule in the Levant, from around 600-1000 C.E. As William Harris notes, varying Christian, Sunni Muslim, and Shia Muslim communities dotted the Levant during this era, but "the peculiarity of Mount Lebanon was the longer-term endurance of a collection of rural sectarian heartlands."[105] After a mélange of rulers and invaders (from the Frankish crusaders to the Mamluks), control of Mount Lebanon and its port cities, by the sixteenth century, fell into Ottoman hands. Throughout the eighteenth and nineteenth centuries, two ascendant ethnic-religious communities emerged in the mountain region: the Druze, who are an offshoot of the Isma'ili Shia sect, and the Maronite Catholics, a Christian sect with an Eastern Catholic religious tradition. Tensions between the two sects culminated in widespread sectarian violence in 1860. These attacks, in effect, "brought another European military intervention and a negotiated new order" within the Ottoman empire.[106] Consequently, an autonomous province of Mount Lebanon was created (the *mutasarrifiya*) with an imperial, non-indigenous governor and a multi-denominational advisory council—a development that marked, as Ussama Makisidi writes, when "Mount Lebanon was communally reinvented," so that "a public and political sectarian identity replaced a nonsectarian politics of notability."[107] The seeds of Lebanon's power-sharing were planted well before the French creation of *Grand Liban*.

The French carved out Greater Lebanon in 1920 from their League of Nations mandate to establish a Christian-majority country. The French justified its suzerainty over this land by asserting a special relationship with the Maronite Catholic people. Thus, the imperial power wished to maintain its traditional ties "especially to the Christians of Lebanon," as "it projected a considerable cultural influence [on] the area."[108] However, in drawing up the borders, French administrators were presented with a

---

[105] William W. Harris, *Lebanon: A History, 600-2011*, Studies in Middle Eastern History (New York, N.Y.) (New York: Oxford University Press, 2012), 30.

[106] Ibid., 148.

[107] Ussama Samir Makdisi, *The Culture of Sectarianism: Community, History, and Violence in Nineteenth-Century Ottoman Lebanon* (Berkeley, California: University of California Press, 2000), 68.

[108] Charles Winslow, *Lebanon: War and Politics in a Fragmented Society* (London; New York: Routledge, 1996), 59.

challenge. As Charles Winslow sums up: "Lebanon needed to be large enough to be economically viable but small enough to make political sense."[109] To solve the dilemma, Mount Lebanon's traditional boundaries were expanded to include many port cities on the Mediterranean, as well as regions to the hinterlands south and east of the mountain range—integrating the ancestral Maronite Catholic and Druze lands with Shia and Sunni Muslim population centers. Lebanon hence became a multi-ethnic, multi-religious state under colonial rule. This inherent friction between the creation of a Western-facing Christian state in the Levant, on the one hand, and the economic considerations of including land with a predominantly Muslim populace who did not identify with the country's cultural-political underpinnings on the other would be *the* fundamental dilemma for Lebanon's national identity.

With French blessings, a constitution was adopted in 1926 and provided the political foundations for the modern-day Lebanese state. The text outlined liberal principles, such as the section on "Individual Rights and Freedoms" that guaranteed the "right against arbitrary arrest or detention," "religious freedom in all its manifestations," and "freedom of education."[110] Also institutionalized was confessional politics, stipulated in Article 95: "religious communities shall be equitably represented in public employment and in the formation of the Cabinet without causing harm to the interests of the State."[111] As Issam Saliba writes, "the deputies have become more the representatives of the religious communities whose seats they occupy rather than representatives of the whole nation or even the geographic districts that elected them."[112] Thus, the Lebanese state during French control formalized the principle of power-sharing via the mechanisms written in its constitution, and in the subsequent decades through legislation, constitutional amendments, and unwritten precedents.

The Second World War proved to be a critical juncture for Lebanon, leading to the country's independence in 1946. During the war, Lebanese

---

[109] Ibid., 61.

[110] Issam Saliba, "Lebanon: Constitutional Law and the Political Rights of Religious Communities," *Library of Congress*, April 2012, https://www.loc.gov/law/help/lebanon/contitutional-law.php, 2.

[111] Ibid., 8.

[112] Ibid.

politicians sought formal independence from French rule through the British, who mediated an agreement between rival ethnic-religious factions to forge a power-sharing government. This was the basis for the 1943 National Pact. British General Edward Spears reached a compromise between the two leading religious sects: the Maronite Catholics, led by Bechara al-Khoury and representing the Christians, and the Sunni Muslims, led by Riad al-Solh and representing the Muslims. Using a 1932 census that showed a slight Christian majority in Lebanon, the two parties agreed to a ratio of six Christian to five Muslim parliamentary seats, solidifying Maronite control of the government. Negotiators agreed to further power-sharing stipulations: a Maronite Catholic would be the country's president, a Sunni Muslim the prime minister, a Shia Muslim the speaker of parliament, and a Greek Orthodox Christian the deputy speaker. This unwritten precedent would guide the infant nation's politics.

The 'National Pact' was born. With al-Khoury as president and al-Solh as prime minister, the governing duo emphasized Lebanon's "Arab face" and a "similar theme of 'no East, no West,' while advocating for a 'special relationship' with the Arab world."[113] Dilip Hiro notes that this political arrangement realigned Lebanese politics from a "Maronite-Druze partnership" to "a Maronite-Sunni alliance," so that "within a generation, modern Lebanon had crystallized as an entity built on the foundation of a confederation of sixteen proto-national communities."[114] With Lebanese independence achieved in 1946, the constitution and the 1943 National Pact enshrined a power-sharing regime for the nation that abided by principles of representative proportionality, which favored Maronite Catholics at the time.

Nevertheless, the 1932 census did not adequately reflect the changing demographic realities in Lebanon. By the mid-twentieth century, the Sunni Muslim population was growing at a faster rate than their Christian compatriots. Rania Maktabi's re-examination of the 1932 census concludes that "the apparent Christian majority in Lebanon was a heavily politicized

---

[113] Farīd al-Ḥāzin, *The Communal Pact of National Identities: The Making and Politics of the 1943 National Pact*, Papers on Lebanon 12 (Oxford: Centre for Lebanese Studies, 1991), 37.

[114] Dilip Hiro, *Lebanon: Fire and Embers : A History of the Lebanese Civil War* (New York: St Martin's Press, 1993), 5.

majority based on the questionable exclusion of considerable numbers of residents on Lebanese territories and the debatable inclusion of significant numbers of emigrants."[115] In essence, the informal pact that crystallized Christian pre-eminence in the Lebanese government clashed with the rising demographic strength and economic aspirations of Muslims in the 1950s. Lebanon's consociational democracy could not withstand internal pressure from the economic and political deprivation of certain ethnic-religious groups, as well as external pressure from the rise of the pan-Arabism and Palestinian resistance movements. Although Marie-Joëlle Zahar identifies the historical factors before Lebanese independence as an example of "one of the most enduring power-sharing experiments," the changing political landscape after independence shook this fundamental element of the polity to its core—and precipitated a civil war in the 1970s.[116]

3.3: *'No Victor, No Vanquished': Civil War and the Road to Peace*

New York Times reporter Thomas Friedman, in his award-winning memoir *From Beirut to Jerusalem*, wrote this of his time spent in the Lebanese capital in 1982: "I don't know if Beirut is a perfect Hobbesian state of nature, but it is probably the closest thing to it that exists in the world today."[117] For his American audience, Beirut represented the 'primordial' nature of the conflicts in the Middle East, where fighters brutally massacred refugees in the name of religion. But for all the reductionist accounts of the Lebanese civil war reproduced in the print media at the time, there were also stories of the complex, multi-level antagonisms that involved sectarian paramilitary groups, the emasculated Lebanese government, the regional powers of Syria and Israel, and the US-led Multi-National Force. Lebanon was a multi-dimensional chess game, and as much as these players wanted to move their pawns—the Lebanese political elite (or the *zu'ama*)—they too knew how to play their players. Figure 6 illustrates the major internal

---

[115] Rania Maktabi, "The Lebanese Census of 1932 Revisited. Who Are the Lebanese?," *British Journal of Middle Eastern Studies* 26, no. 2 (1999): 219–41, 240.

[116] See Marie-Joëlle Zahar, "Power Sharing in Lebanon: Foreign Protectors, Domestic Peace, and Democratic Failure" in Roeder and Rothchild, *Sustainable Peace.*

[117] Friedman, *From Beirut to Jerusalem: Updated with a New Chapter* (New York: Anchor Books, Doubleday, 1995), 30.

players during the war. This table is not comprehensive; it becomes all too apparent after studying the civil war that this is as simple as I can get to devising a neat configuration of the factions in the Lebanese civil war.

Figure 6. Political and Military Actors during the Lebanese Civil War (1975-1989)

Religion	Christians			Muslims			Druze
Sect	Maronite Catholic	Greek Orthodox	Sunni		Shia		N/A
Armed Group	Phalange (*Kataeb*)	Lebanese Forces	N/A	*Al-Mourabitoun* (Independent Nasserites)	Amal Movement	Hezbollah	Progressive Socialist Party

There are many historical and political studies that look into the causes of the Lebanese civil war. For this work, however, I will focus on the effect the war had on the ruling political class. The figure above provides a glimpse into the environment that the Taif Accords was negotiated in. During the conflict, sectarian paramilitary groups provided security and aid while they controlled territories throughout the country, because of the anemic Lebanese state. The primary factor that precipitated the conflict was, as Hiro describes, "the perception shared by the Maronite leadership that the presence of the Palestine commandos in Lebanon was a serious threat to Lebanese sovereignty."[118] Christian, Muslim, and Druze mobilized on ethnic-religious lines. Sectarian paramilitary groups flourished as they defended their territorial claims. Within each sect, personality-led divisions fragmented ethnic groups, resulting in a multiple-actor conflict within each sectarian grouping. Any attempt to negotiate between paramilitary groups and/or the government seemed futile, because

---

[118] Hiro, *Lebanon*, 20.

"conflict regulation broke down when one of the Lebanese communities or actors operated their strategy in an attempt to get more than a relative advantage" over the political situation.[119] By viewing this civil war not as an inherently religious conflict but rather a more traditional one over resources, power, and legitimacy among a multiplicity of local actors (with the support of external interferences) we can analyze the Taif agreement through our theoretical lens from Chapter 2.

3.4: *The Taif Accords: A Projection of Possibilities or Political Compromise?*

The Taif Accords—named after the Saudi Arabian city where it was brokered—was ratified on November 4, 1989 by the Lebanese parliament, giving greater political representation and power for Muslims in Lebanon after a grueling fifteen-year civil war. The concept of consociational democracy, once implicit in the 1943 National Pact, was now spelled out in this constitutional overhaul. Theodor Hanf observes this new reality: "In the Taif Agreement, coexistence between the religious communities is solemnly affirmed, declared the foundation of Lebanese legality and, more explicitly than ever before, recognized as both the state's raison d'étre and its objective."[120] During the civil war, various factions supported breaking up Lebanon into separate nation-states corresponding to homogeneous ethnic homelands—in essence, a partition of the country. The Taif Accords dismissed those notions, choosing to maintain the viability of the Lebanese state through a foundational principle of coexistence. Certainly, a lofty goal for a society ravaged by internal strife. In Figure 7, I summarize my textual analysis of the Taif Accords, categorizing each section into the SSI and cohesion strategies framework.

---

[119] Theodor Hanf, *Coexistence in Wartime Lebanon: Decline of a State and Rise of a Nation* (London: Centre for Lebanese Studies in association with IBTauris, 1993), 140.
[120] Ibid., 585.

Figure 7. Sites of Social Interaction (SSIs) and Cohesion Strategies in the Taif Accords

Section of Taif Accords	Site(s) of Social Interaction	Cohesion Strategy	Summary of textual analysis
General Principles	Coexistence	Assimilation and Differentiation	Commitment to "coexistence" of religious sects, reaffirmation of state's overall Arab identity, and emphasis on economic justice and reform for all religious sects.
Political Institutions	Contestation	Differentiation	Executive roles designated to specific sects increased Sunni Muslim power at the cost of Maronite Catholics and distributed parliamentary seats in proportion to sects (1:1 Christian to Muslim ratio)
Education/ Displacement	Collaboration	Assimilation and Differentiation	National curriculum meant to unify and cultivate national identity, state to facilitate the return of displaced to pre-war homes
Cultural/ Religious	Coexistence	Differentiation	Religious leaders' prerogatives over community members' "personal status," right of each community's religious practices and education.

Overall Agreement	Coexistence	Assimilation and Differentiation	Agreement has contradictory strategic goals, but envisions a national identity based on the principle of coexistence as expressed in "General Principles."

In its "General Principles and Reforms," the agreement reaffirmed Lebanon's 'Arab face' according to sub-section B, in which "Lebanon is Arab in belonging and identity."[121] Instead of being a bastion of Western civilization in the Near East, the Lebanese state would place itself among other Arab nations and share in the region's identity. The agreement outlined a Lebanese identity that emphasized its Arab roots in a strategy of assimilating all ethnic groups in a 'common denominator' identity. Sprinkled in this first section are references to economic and social justice, describing that while "the economic system is a free system that guarantees individual initiative and private ownership," the state would make an effort "to achieve comprehensive social justice through fiscal, economic, and social reform."[122] These statements allude to the economic grievances of Lebanese Muslims in the 1970s, and particularly the poverty of the Shia population. Musa al-Sadr would successfully mobilize the poverty-stricken Shia with the "Movement of the Dispossessed" (*Harakat al-Mahrumin*) during the war.[123] The last sub-section makes it clear that the Taif Accords will adhere to a cohesion strategy of differentiation: "No authority violating the common co-existence charter shall be legitimate."[124] The golden rule of coexistence is a forthright project, and the agreement even stipulates that it is the principle that legitimizes the Lebanese state. In short, the aspirational "General Principles" of Taif highlight the power-sharing agreement's strategy of assimilation and differentiation through sites of coexistence—that is, in theory.

---

[121] "Taif Accords | UN Peacemaker," accessed January 4, 2021, https://peacemaker.un.org/lebanon-taifaccords89, 1.

[122] Ibid.

[123] "Roots of the Shi'i Movement," MERIP, June 24, 1985, https://merip.org/1985/06/roots-of-the-shii-movement/.

[124] "Taif Accords," 1.

A whole host of political reforms reconfigure the Chamber of Deputies in the second section of Taif so that Christians and Muslims are equally represented. Most of the Maronite Catholic president's prerogatives are transferred to an empowered Sunni Muslim prime minister. In subsection five, the parliament is divvied up "equally between Christians and Muslims," "proportionately between the denominations of each sect," and "proportionately between the districts."[125] This contrasts with the National Pact's six to five ratio of parliamentary representation because the power-sharing agreement rearranges the division of power so that Muslims have a greater say in the legislature. To achieve this, negotiators had to increase the number of seats in parliament, so during talks, it was proposed to raise it from 99 to 128. The political elites—who mainly sat out of the conflict or derived power as the traditional, notable *zu'ama* class—feared "this would enable too many militia leaders and warlords—and Syrian clients—to enter parliament."[126] So the delegates compromised with 108 seats, "the minimum number needed to create parity without depriving the Christians of existing seats."[127] Moreover, executive power was shifted from the president to a Cabinet headed by the prime minister, relegating the president to the status of a figurehead.[128] These compromises, though orchestrated by the remaining parliamentarians of the 1972 Chamber of Deputies, were greatly facilitated by the 'troika' of Saudi Arabia, Morocco, and Algeria. And all of this politicking happened under the shadow of the Syrian occupation. In line with theories of consociational democracy, the equality of Christian and Muslim representation was supposed to foster grand coalition building in the Cabinet. The political apparatus became a site of contestation for ethnic factions in a legal framework designed to moderate winning or losing in theory, in the hope of coalition politics.

Other provisions in the Taif document cover religious autonomy, education, and civil war displacement. Under Section III, sub-section B2 the "heads of the Lebanese sects" have constitutional prerogatives over one's personal status, "the practice of religious rites" and the "freedom of

---

125 Ibid., 2.

126 Hanf, *Coexistence*, 586.

127 Ibid.

128 See "General Principles and Reforms" Section II, sub-sections B, C, and D in "Taif Accords."

religious education."[129] Sub-section F deals with the state of education in the country: it guarantees free and obligatory education "for the elementary stage at least," strengthens state control over private schools and textbooks, emphasizes vocational education and reforms at the Lebanese University, and mandated a revised national curricula "that strengthens national belonging, fusion, spiritual and cultural openness...on the subjects of history and national education."[130] The issue of displacement during the civil war is addressed as well. Taif establishes "the right of every Lebanese evicted since 1975 to return to the place from which he was evicted" and that "legislation to guarantee this right and to ensure the means of reconstruction shall be issued."[131] These three sections are attempts to codify social and cultural reforms for the new Lebanese government, and address issues of segmental autonomy for "internal affairs"—in this case, the autonomy of the religious sects—that Lijphart constitutes as a key aspect of consociationalism.[132] Through these specific sections, efforts are made to cultivate sites of collaboration through education and the return of the displaced, and sites of coexistence for religious practices. Both cohesion strategies of differentiation, represented by the right to return to pre-1975 homes (many of which were mixed neighborhoods), and assimilation, via a national curriculum, are pursued. Thus, Taif produces social, cultural, and economic sites of coexistence and collaboration, with the cohesion strategies of differentiation and national assimilation in these areas of Lebanese society.

Lastly, Taif formalizes the Syrian army's presence in the country, outlines a process for demilitarization, and calls on Israel's withdrawal from the south. It is apparent that the last three sections of the treaty address the country's foreign occupation by Syria and Israel—and reflects the role of external powers in both stabilizing and destabilizing the Lebanese state. Provisions detail that all Lebanese and non-Lebanese militias should disband, and their weapons "delivered to the State of Lebanon within a period of 6 months" after the charter's ratification.[133] The main enforcer

---

[129] "Taif Accords," 6.
[130] Ibid., 6-7.
[131] Ibid., 7.
[132] Lijphart, *Democracy*, 25.
[133] "Taif Accords," 7.

would be Syrian president Hafez al-Assad and his army: "the Syrian forces shall thankfully assist the forces of the legitimate Lebanese government to spread the authority of the State of Lebanon with a set period of no more than 2 years."[134] This acknowledges the reality on the ground in Lebanon by the end of the civil war. The agreement then calls for the end of the Israeli occupation. Lebanon, according to Taif, will "[take] all the steps necessary to liberate all Lebanese territories from the Israeli occupation" and "deploy the Lebanese army in the border area adjacent to Israel."[135] The last section effectively condones Syrian suzerainty over Lebanon, citing that "between Lebanon and Syria there is a special relationship that derives its strength from the roots of blood relationships, history, and joint fraternal interests."[136] Al-Assad received international acknowledgment of his control over Lebanon, a remarkable feat considering that Saddam Hussein's invasion of Kuwait just months after the Taif Accords received a multinational rebuke and a UN military response.

Though unpalatable to many Lebanese, these provisions in the Taif were nonnegotiable. Prince Saud al-Faisal of Saudi Arabia implored delegates to approve the treaty and painted a dark picture if they could not come to compromise: "He reminded them of the rejection of the United Nations plan for the partition of Palestine in 1947; the Palestinians were still searching for a bit of land. The Lebanese, too, were in danger of becoming a homeless people."[137] These portions of the agreement further solidify the argument that external powers can stabilize ethnic civil wars through hegemonic control.

Reading between the lines, the Taif agreement was meant to be a framework to transition from a confessional government similar to the 1926 constitution but with Christian-Muslim parity, to an eventual non-sectarian government. Fawwaz Tarabulsi acknowledges this possibility in Taif, that "the Second Republic it gave birth to was to lead to a Third Republic in which political sectarianism would be abolished," but he tempers this idealism in the document with this point: "In practical terms, the Ta'if regime reproduced the sectarian system, but with a sizeable

---

[134] Ibid., 8.
[135] Ibid.
[136] Ibid.
[137] Hanf, *Coexistence*, 589.

modification in the balance of power among its constituents."[138] The political arrangements evened the playing field for Muslims in government, rectifying a major cause of the Lebanese civil war. The sites of contestation, in the form of government, seemed to balance political power, reflecting a moderation of Christian power and bolstering of Muslim power.

As for the sections regarding religion, education, and displacement, a 'top-down' attempt was made to institute programs to cultivate sites of coexistence and collaboration. A product of compromise, the Taif agreement had seemingly contradictory strategies for power-sharing: in one line, the document pursues a differentiation strategy through "coexistence," while in another, it pursues assimilation through de-sectarianizing the political constitution of the state as a "fundamental national objective." An analysis of Lebanon's history after Taif will help clarify what these abstract principles really meant in practice and if ethnic tensions did increase or decrease as a result of the provisions in this power-sharing arrangement.

Figure 8. Lebanon Predicted Outcomes

Overall Agreement	Coexistence	Assimilation and Differentiation	Hypothetical Analysis
Predicted Ethnic Tensions	Increase/ Decrease	Increase and Increase/ Decrease	On balance, more factors indicate a likely increase rather than decrease in ethnic tension
Predicted Power-Sharing Outcome	Limited Failure/ Limited Success	Failure and Limited Failure/ Limited Success	On balance, more factors indicate power-sharing failure/limited failure rather than limited success/ success

---

[138] Fawwāz Ṭarābulsī, *A History of Modern Lebanon*, Second edition. (New York, NY, London: Palgrave Macmillian, Pluto Press, 2012), 250.

3.5: *Lebanon After Taif: An Agreement Faces a Tough Reality*

Lebanese politicians faced a formidable trade-off after the Taif accords. On the one hand, the state must consolidate its new power-sharing government and rebuild a war-weary society. On the other, the Lebanese had to face the prospect of Syrian political meddling. So long as the Syrian intelligence apparatus was monitoring Beirut and military installations were kept throughout the country, Hafez al-Assad would have the final say in political matters. Indeed, through subsequent treaties, "the Syrian hold on Lebanon was fully institutionalized," as Rola el-Husseini and Ryan Crocker contend.[139] However, a military commander—with the backing of a populist Christian movement—would not have any of that.

After the treaty's ratification, the self-styled 'Gaullist' General Michel Aoun asserted his legitimacy as president by refusing to concede to Syrian occupation, holding out in the presidential palace at Baabda. Over time, however, the general's opposition to the Taif agreement and Syrian occupation was met with Syrian-backed politicians in the new 'National Accord' government: "the [Elias] Hrawi-[Selim] Hoss administration attempted to show that it was on top of its problems and that the Taif Accord was being implemented."[140] In October 1990, Aoun's movement was forcefully squashed by both the Central Bank's refusal to pay his shadow government's employees in addition to the Syrian army's military operation forcing Aoun out of the Baabda palace. For his part, Aoun's movement fizzled out as the general went into exile in France.

This incident shows how the Syrians acted as a peacekeeping force with tacit Arab League support through Taif. With this stabilizing presence, president Hrawi intended to form a Cabinet that would incentivize paramilitary demilitarization, by "[providing] seats to militia leaders as a reward for disbanding their forces."[141] Although the Israeli occupation remained unsolved in the south, most militias laid down their arms in accordance with the power-sharing agreement. Their leaders, like Nabih

---

[139] Rola el-Husseini and Ryan Crocker, "The Lebanese Political System: The Elite Pacts of 1943 and 1989," in *Pax Syriana*, Elite Politics in Postwar Lebanon (Syracuse University Press, 2012), 1–22, https://www.jstor.org/stable/j.ctt1j1nvk4.7, 17.

[140] Hiro, *Lebanon*, 172.

[141] Ibid., 186.

Berri and Walid Jumblatt, were integrated into the government as high-ranking portfolio ministers. However, one militia based in southern Lebanon, and deriving its support from the Shia population and Iran, did not de-commission because it claimed to continue the 'resistance' against Israel—Hezbollah. This group, which perpetrated the US Marine barracks attack in 1983, 'rebranded' themselves as a "resistance force," rather than a militia, and was never de-mobilized.[142] This adds another layer of complexity to Lebanon's political situation down the road. As Samantha May explains, the failure to demobilize Hezbollah "has created the conditions that have eroded the Lebanese state's monopoly of violence both within and without Lebanese territory" today.[143] But on balance, peace in Lebanon seemed like a real possibility in the aftermath of the Taif agreement.

After fifteen years of relative peace, the tumult of the 2005 assassination of Rafik Hariri, the 'Cedar Revolution,' and the Syrian army's withdrawal from Lebanon marked a critical juncture for the country's fragile power-sharing institutions. During the 1990s and early 2000s, prime minister Rafik Hariri oversaw Lebanon's economic recovery, rebuilding Beirut and introducing neoliberal economic reforms. All of this was facilitated by Hariri's connections to the Gulf states, because prior to his political career, he was a construction tycoon in Saudi Arabia. In addition, his "monopolization of Sunni institutions and marginalization of potential competitors" in Lebanon through his charitable foundation solidified his grip in politics, as Melani Cammett and Sukriti Issar underscore.[144] Hariri's soaring popularity and cold relations with Bashar al-Assad made the prime minister a threat to Syrian hegemony in Lebanon by the early 2000s. On February 14, 2005, an explosion killed Hariri as his motorcade drove past the St. George Hotel in Beirut. Amidst international outcry and speculations that the Syrian regime orchestrated the assassination,

---

[142] Samantha May, "The Rise of the 'Resistance Axis': Hezbollah and the Legacy of the Taif Agreement," *Nationalism and Ethnic Politics* 25, no. 1 (January 2, 2019): 115–32, https://doi.org/10.1080/13537113.2019.1565184, 125.

[143] Ibid., 127.

[144] Melani Cammett and Sukriti Issar, "Bricks and Mortar Clientelism: Sectarianism and the Logics of Welfare Allocation in Lebanon," *World Politics* 62, no. 3 (July 2010): 381–421, https://doi.org/10.1017/S0043887110000080, 400.

demonstrators protested against the pro-Syrian government led by president Émile Lahoud and newly-appointed prime minister Omar Karami. What they did not anticipate was that Hariri's death would electrify the Lebanese people—and cause the peaceful withdrawal of Syrian troops long overdue under Taif's terms.

The Cedar Revolution—as Western media labeled it—resulted in a political realignment in Lebanon between multi-religious blocs in favor and opposed to Syrian withdrawal—named after the day of each side's demonstrations, March 14 and March 8 blocs, respectively. Andrew Arsan portrays the spirit of the Lebanese protestors: "Loudly proclaiming its opposition to Syria's presence in Lebanon, 14 March has presented itself as the guarantor not just of the country's independence and sovereignty, but also of its stability" while "8 March has portrayed itself as part of a regional 'axis' ranged against the forces of Western neo-imperialism, Zionism, and Sunni jihadi obscurantism."[145] Eventually, sectarian affiliation came to the forefront, as the Sunni Future Movement party (*al-Mustaqbal*), led by Saad Hariri (son of Rafik Hariri), sided with the Maronite Lebanese Forces leader Samir Geagea in the anti-Syrian alliance, while Shia Amal and Hezbollah entered into an agreement with the Maronite Free Patriotic Movement in the pro-Syrian bloc—spearheaded, ironically, by Michel Aoun. In this scenario, Christians as an ethnic community held the balance of power amongst the division between Sunni and Shia Muslims. Coalesced behind pro- and anti-Syrian stances, ethnic tensions between Christian, Sunni, and Shia sects simmered as Lebanon faced a precarious position and a potential for renewed political violence.

Animosities came to a boiling point on May 7, 2008, when the March 8 bloc mobilized Shia militiamen from Amal, Hezbollah, and the Syrian Socialist National Party (SSNP) and paralyzed the streets of Beirut, when the government attempted to dismiss the pro-Hezbollah head of security at the international airport and dismantle a private, Hezbollah-built communications network.[146] Sunni Future Movement and Druze PSP

---

[145] Andrew Arsan, *Lebanon: A Country in Fragments* (London: Hurst & Company, 2018), 7-8.

[146] Nada Bakri and Alan Cowell, "Lebanese Reach Agreement to Resolve 18-Month Political Crisis," *The New York Times*, May 21, 2008, https://www.nytimes.com/2008/05/21/world/africa/21iht-lebanon.4.13105564.html.

members of the March 14 bloc responded by mobilizing their own partisans, and light skirmishes occurred throughout the capital. However, as Sami Hermez chronicles, "the Christian factions were not openly involved," most likely, because of their interethnic division in the political blocs.[147] Lebanon came at the cliff's edge of civil war. The Arab League, under the guidance of the Qatari emir, summoned parties for a "National Dialogue" in Doha, in which they agreed to a political settlement and the end of the armed crisis. A consensus candidate, General Michel Sleiman, would be elected as Lebanese president while a new "Government of national unity" would increase the pro-Hezbollah opposition's representation and give them a veto.[148] In addition, both sides agreed on "an electoral law that divides the country into smaller-sized political districts that will influence the outcome of the next parliamentary elections in 2009."[149] Hezbollah and its allies effectively harnessed their 'resistance' militia to capture power through Lebanon's political institutions, creating favorable conditions for them to gain a greater say in politics undemocratically. But the Taif Accords technically remained intact. These two blocs, in alliance to this day, remain committed to the confessional system.

The first twenty years of Lebanon's reconstituted government show that there was only a partial implementation of the Taif Accords. Both the historical record and political analysis confirm the power-sharing arrangement's rocky start. Figure 9 depicts the Taif Accord's so-called "progress report" in regard to its implementation. I compile the University of Notre Dame's *Peace Accords Matrix* data on Lebanon's power-sharing agreement to chart its implementation by section of the text. I select ten aspects of the agreement that the dataset codes for in both the Taif and

---

[147] Sami Hermez, *War Is Coming: Between Past and Future Violence in Lebanon*, The Ethnography of Political Violence (Philadelphia: University of Pennsylvania Press, Inc, University of Pennsylvania Press, 2017), 87.

[148] "Doha Agreement on the Results of the Lebanese National Dialogue Conference | UN Peacemaker," accessed January 4, 2021, https://peacemaker.un.org/lebanon-dohaagreement2008, 1.

[149] Brenda Ghazzar, "Politicians hope Doha agreement, Suleiman election will end violence," *The Jerusalem Post*, May 26, 2008, https://advance-lexis-com.proxy.bc.edu/api/document?collection=news&id=urn:contentItem: 53Y6-YJH1-F12G-D55K-00000-00&context=1516831.

Good Friday Agreements and provide the overall implementation score. An analysis of the GFA's score will occur in Chapter 4. As for Lebanon, ten years since Taif was enacted, there was an only partial implementation of the overall agreement. Two spheres, mentioned previously in my text analysis of the Taif agreement, are worth highlighting in the *Peace Accords Matrix*. Education reform received a "no implementation" code and economic and social development received a "minimum implementation" code. To understand why this is the case, I analyze Lebanon's education system and economic/displacement policies after peace was achieved in 1989 to determine how (or if) the SSIs and cohesion strategies in Taif were implemented and their impact on ethnic tensions within these spheres.

Figure 9. Implementation of Taif Accords 10 Years After Adoption[150]

Taif Accords (1989-1997)	*Implementation*
Power-sharing Transitional Government	Full Implementation
Electoral/Political Party Reform	Intermediate Implementation
Decentralization/Federalism	No Implementation
Dispute Resolution Committee	Full Implementation
Judiciary Reform	Full Implementation
Paramilitary Groups	Intermediate Implementation

[150] Data from Madhav Joshi, Jason Michael Quinn, and Patrick M Regan, "Annualized Implementation Data on Comprehensive Intrastate Peace Accords, 1989–2012," *Journal of Peace Research* 52, no. 4 (2015): 551–62, https://doi.org/10.1177/0022343314567486.

Education Reform	No Implementation
Economic and Social Development	Minimum Implementation
Detailed Implementation Timeline	Intermediate Implementation
Taif Accords overall implementation score (out of 100)	**59.26**

3.6: *Lebanese Education: A Lost Opportunity*

Implicit in Lebanon's power-sharing agreement is the willingness of political elites to harness the Lebanese education system to cultivate a shared national identity. It envisions education as a site of collaboration between various sects to further a cohesion strategy of assimilation. In reality, subsequent steps by the government, religious leaders, and other political actors derailed the possibility of forging a truly shared national curriculum. Coupled with the deteriorating socio-political and economic situation in the country in the mid-2000s and 2010s, the Lebanese government has failed to foster collaboration and assimilation in education. It is no surprise, then, to see that education reform is coded as "no implementation" in the *Peace Accords Matrix*. Instead, education remains a site of contestation; inequal among sects, and rife with ethnic tension—especially in the subjects of civics and history. For a new, post-conflict generation of Lebanese students, the classroom can be a minefield that can trigger group animosities.

As mentioned earlier, Section III F of the Taif agreement deals with education, in addition to Section III B, 2.3, which explicitly accounts for a "freedom of religious education."[151] In accordance with the treaty and the new government's economic plan, the 1994 Education Recovery Plan charged the Education Center for Research and Development (ECRD) with developing a new curriculum and school assessment criteria. Nemer

---

[151] "Taif Accords," 6 and 7.

Frayha, a leading scholar in education, was tasked as the head of the ECRD from 1999 to 2002. His unique account of his time as a leading policymaker in post-Taif Lebanon—writing through the lens of both theorist and practitioner—helps in understanding the political dynamics at play during his tenure. For instance, Frayha was keenly aware of "the larger configurations of power operating within Lebanese society," and was "[determined] to act as a specialized scholar rather than a public relations figure," especially when he embarked to overhaul the state curriculum.[152] However, his idealism was soon tempered by the political forces surrounding him: "In hindsight…as ECRD director, I really had little room to maneuver given the power wielded by pressure groups."[153] Considering this, reformist and integrationist elements in Lebanese society failed to consolidate against traditional religious-political groups to produce a unifying national curriculum.

The Lebanese education system has been the mainstay of private institutions—most notably, religious groups—because the public school system had been weak and underdeveloped, even before the civil war. This had to do with the religious lobby and its vested interest in molding the minds of its believers. Frayha contends that religious leaders "tend to consider education as a particularly sensitive area worthy of their attention, especially since they run a large number of private schools and universities."[154] The outsized influence of religious sects in the schools is glaring. Over 40% of higher education institutions are either predominantly Christian or Muslim.[155] The power of the sectarian political machine is immense in education policy, as "religious leaders have access to the grass roots, and the ability to mobilize the masses in favor or against a particular policy initiative."[156] For his part, Frayha was determined to use a "unified history" and the "writing of civics textbooks" to contribute to Lebanon's

---

[152] Nemer Frayha, "Pressure Groups, Education Policy, and Curriculum Development in Lebanon: A Policymaker's Retrospective and Introspective Standpoint," *Education and the Arab "World": Political Projects, Struggles, and Geometries of Power*, 95.

[153] Ibid., 97.

[154] Ibid., 98.

[155] "In Lebanon, a University Unites a Fragmented Society," accessed February 15, 2021, https://www.chronicle.com/article/in-lebanon-a-university-unites-a-fragmented-society/.

[156] Frayha, "Pressure Groups," 98.

post-conflict reconciliation.[157] With this in mind, the 1994 Education Recovery Plan empowered the ECRD to overhaul the Lebanese education system and construct a new curriculum, with the goal of cultivating national unity and assimilating pupils under a common Lebanese banner. Ideally, Frayha intended for a site of collaboration to take root, which would aid in socializing young citizens into a truly national identity.

At first, the Plan for Educational Reform showed promise in its stated objectives, opting to carry out the explicit and implicit sentiments of the Taif Accords by enacting a cohesion strategy of assimilation by way of a site of collaboration. The plan "locates the humanistic and religious dimensions of education as the basis of learning aims and activities," synthesizing Lebanese secularists' liberal, pluralistic vision and traditional Lebanese religious leaders' concern for religion as a basis for educating.[158] Key principles are enumerated in the document, such as:

"Principle 5:
The formation of a citizen who:

(a) Feels honoured in his country–Lebanon–and is proud of his loyalty and belonging to it.

(b) Is proud of his Arab identity and kinship, and of his commitment to them.

(c) Recognizes the long national Lebanese history that, emancipated from extremist beliefs, will attain a unified, open and humanistic society.

(d) Realizes the importance of co-existence among all citizens since 'there is no legality for any authority that contradicts the Document of Co-existence', which remains a unique guide in the region and to the whole world.

(e) Respects personal and social freedom and preserves others' rights and properties."[159]

---

[157] Ibid., 104.

[158] Nemer Frayha, "Education and Social Cohesion in Lebanon," *Prospects* 33, no. 1 (March 1, 2003): 77–88, https://doi.org/10.1023/A:1022664415479, 85.

[159] Ibid.

These propositions indicate a concerted effort, by scholars and policymakers, to cultivate a unified Lebanese nationalism inclusive of all religious sects. In this context, assimilation is achieved under an umbrella 'nationalism' defined by Lebanon's status as an Arab nation that nevertheless subscribes to liberal principles of tolerance.

Since the 1994 Education Recovery Plan introduced a national history textbook in 1997 two more attempts to revise the curriculum (2000 and 2012) failed due to the issue's perceived divisiveness as ethnic tensions became more fraught in Lebanon. The 1997 textbook, as Maha Shuayb observes, "shows the big emphasis placed on nation building, unity and the Lebanese identity as means for building peace and social cohesion."[160] This revamp in the public education sector was meant to address the political reformation of a post-war generation in Lebanon. Forging a national Lebanese identity corresponded to creating a curriculum that included an over-arching Lebanese history that explains the civil war era. This contrasts to fragmented historical accounts, seen in many divided societies, that attribute blame or wrongdoing to a particular sect—thus informing one's views of the other. It is, of course, a challenging feat—and sectarian groups could not agree to this history. This affected the educational reform as it "was highly inclusive of various religious, sectarian and economic sectors in Lebanon," but not "students and parents."[161] Opting for a top-down approach to state curricula, subsequent reforms to the textbooks stalled as the political environment fractured in the mid-2000s. Thus, it was evident that the religious establishment would not relinquish their hold on their privileges in the realm of education.

As the Lebanese public education system deteriorated in the 2010s, the gap between public and private schools widened. This has led to a serious divergence in Lebanese history and civics education. Bassel Akar and Mara Albrecht conducted an empirical analysis on civics education in Lebanese private schools. They found that "classroom reflections suggested dominant didactic pedagogies for the purpose of students passing exams and degrees of resistance towards classroom discussions so as to avoid conflicts with

---

[160] Maha Shuayb, "Education for Social Cohesion Attempts in Lebanon: Reflections on the 1994 and 2010 Education Reforms," *Education as Change* 20, no. 3 (2016): 225–42, https://doi.org/10.17159/1947-9417/2016/1531, 233.

[161] Ibid., 237.

and among students."[162] The collaborative site Frayha conceived gave way to a fraught atmosphere, where difficult conversations about religion and conflict are sidestepped. Pedantic approaches to the subject of civics are adopted as it creates the least controversy, in comparison to 'active' learning.

Another issue is the proliferation of private schools after the civil war and well into the twenty-first century that are registered as foreign programs (e.g. the French *baccalauréat* system). Foreign-accredited schools have a high degree of autonomy and do not adhere to the national curriculum on civics.[163] Akar and Albrecht estimate that "just over half" of Lebanese pupils registered in private schools do not learn through the state curriculum—a worrying sign, as the schools they studied "are recognized as among the most elite private institutions in Lebanon."[164] They also report how the supposed national education was in practice just rote memorization. As one teacher complains, "the other subjects I teach, like history and geography, [students] don't like them because they're dry. And civics is even drier…because there is no understanding, all memorisation."[165] A serious dilemma emerges because the unifying education first proposed in Taif and implemented by legislation is not even taught to a sizeable population of students. In their investigation, the researchers conclude:

> "Findings from empirical studies suggest that the implementation of these nationalist aims in Lebanon as a framework for policy (curricular design and textbooks) and practices (classroom learning) generates degrees of social exclusion and barriers to learning active citizenship and history as a discipline."[166]

The evidence thus points out that the national Lebanese curriculum has mainly failed in cultivating the sites of collaboration it had once

---

[162] Bassel Akar and Mara Albrecht, "Influences of Nationalisms on Citizenship Education: Revealing a 'Dark Side' in Lebanon," *Nations and Nationalism* 23, no. 3 (2017): 547–70, https://doi.org/10.1111/nana.12316, 555.
[163] Ibid., 557-8.
[164] Ibid., 558.
[165] Ibid., 560.
[166] Ibid., 561.

promised. Instead, an increasing number of students in the 2010s are not even exposed to the state textbooks—a form of social exclusion. It seems that education is viewed as a site of coexistence, at best, or a site of contestation, at worst.

Public schools, which do teach the national curriculum, are usually representative of homogenized communities, meaning that these spaces lack the necessary conditions for collaboration between ethnic groups. Hoda Baytiyeh stresses how demography shapes the learning experience for students when administrators, teachers, and fellow classmates come from the same religious sect. "Despite the fact that these public schools commonly encourage national patriotism along with religious inspiration, such segregation in public education prevents social interaction between students required to overcome narrow views," she concludes.[167] There is still no agreed-upon history curriculum in Lebanon, so the subject "…is taught in schools on the basis of the 1971 pre-civil war curriculum that, evidently, lacks any reference to events that are key to understanding present-day Lebanon."[168] This national amnesia reflects how contested the civil war history is, and what is at stake in teaching history in the country. In general, politics in the classroom is strictly shunned. As Erik van Ommering puts it, "[teachers] resorted to neglecting the topic of war and violence altogether and complained about students being obsessed with sectarianism and politics."[169] These elements in schooling combine to reveal a bleak picture, as the vision of education in Taif as a tool for assimilation and a site for collaboration has yet to be fully manifested in Lebanon. Rather, the schoolyard is a contested space for ethnic-religious groups.

An educational divide in Lebanon is persistent between Muslims and Christians. A recent study by Rania Tfaily, Hassan Diab, and Andrzej Kulcycki uses an innovative empirical model to examine educational

---

[167] Hoda Baytiyeh, "Has the Educational System in Lebanon Contributed to the Growing Sectarian Divisions?," *Education and Urban Society* 49, no. 5 (June 1, 2017): 546–59, https://doi.org/10.1177/0013124516645163, 553.

[168] Erik van Ommering, "Schooling in Conflict: An Ethnographic Study from Lebanon," ed. Madeleine Leonard, Martina McKnight, and Spyros Spyrou, *International Journal of Sociology and Social Policy* 31, no. 9/10 (January 1, 2011): 543–54, https://doi.org/10.1108/01443331111164133, 547.

[169] Ibid., 549.

disparities by religious sect. Their findings confirm that there are gaps not only between communities, but also in geographic distribution throughout Lebanon. School enrollment for Sunni and Shia Muslims outside of Beirut lagged behind Christians, and even Sunni Muslims in Tripoli and Saida "were significantly disadvantaged."[170] Geographical divides in communities are also present: Christian education was "considerably lower" among Christians in the south and Bekaa valley, and Shia Muslims in the south were more educated than those in the Bekaa.[171] They conclude that "the regional/sectarian disparities that pre-dated the civil war were still to a large extent replicated in the current analysis, especially for men."[172] These empirical data analyses support the claim that Lebanon's education system has ultimately failed to live up to its promise in Taif—to strengthen "national belonging, fusion, spiritual and cultural openness" as a site of collaboration.[173]

Equipped with the knowledge of the political landscape in Lebanon after the Cedar Revolution, it comes to no surprise that the Lebanese education system is failing in its purpose to assimilate the population under a broad national identity. Education, envisioned as a site of collaboration in Taif, is undermined by political intransigence and educational inequalities. This, in turn, exacerbates religious and class divides. The power-sharing attempt to bring about a site of collaboration, in this instance, has failed—and the potential for education to decrease ethnic tensions has diminished. Education is practically a site of contestation for the country, in which political actors try to gain leverage over other ethnic groups, thereby making the topics of history and civics hotly-contested issues.

3.7: *The Demographic Spheres of Beirut: A Microcosm of Lebanese Displacement*

It is hard to understand Lebanon without understanding its capital city, Beirut. A microcosm of the country's ethnic diversity and outward-facing

---

[170] Rania Tfaily, Hassan Diab, and Andrzej Kulczycki, "Educational Disparities and Conflict: Evidence from Lebanon," *Research in Comparative and International Education* 8, no. 1 (March 1, 2013): 55–73, https://doi.org/10.2304/rcie.2013.8.1.55, 66.

[171] Ibid., 67.

[172] Ibid., 69.

[173] "Taif Accords," 7.

culture, the city has weathered through colonization, occupation, civil war, economic turmoil, and political unrest. This section will discuss the effects of post-war reconstruction on displacement and economic inequality. A disconnect between the treaty's language and the post-war Lebanese government's orientation towards development in Beirut resulted in reinforcing, rather than weakening, ethnic division in the capital— thereby transforming a proposed site of coexistence and collaboration into a site of contestation. An avenue for economic justice after the civil war, the displacement clause in Taif was tainted by corruption, so that family housing claims were bought out by a pseudo-public-private corporation, Solidere. This exasperated sectarian animosities as it resulted in the literal destruction of the pre-war city center into a place wiped away (or sterilized, if put more bluntly) of Lebanon's bloody past.

If one views Beirut's reconstruction through the lens of the Taif agreement's Guiding Principles and Displacement clauses, then one sees the capital's physical and demographic landscape attest to the promise of power-sharing and the ultimate pitfalls of the post-war peace in Lebanon. Three points in Taif's "General Principles" outline the state's commitment to; (1) a "free" economic system and "private ownership," (2) a "culturally, socially, and economically-balanced development," and (3) an effort to achieve "social justice" through reform.[174] Further, Section D, pertaining to "spreading the sovereignty of the State of Lebanon" addresses the war.[175] It establishes the right for Lebanese citizens to return to their pre-war homes.[176] These provisions envision a site of coexistence and collaboration, in which ethnic groups could possibly share more equitably in the economic 'pie' and return to some pre-war neighborhoods with mixed religious sects. This demonstrates an assimilation and differentiation strategy, in which a national effort to revitalize the economy would unify the Lebanese and tolerance would underpin sectarian intermixing in pre-war neighborhoods.

Before the civil war, Beirut reflected a site of coexistence, in which ethnic groups co-inhabited in the same city, but in different neighborhoods. Jon Calame and Esther Ruth Charlesworth recount the history of Beirut's demographic landscape, noting that the city "traditionally functioned

---

[174] Ibid., 1.

[175] Ibid., 7.

[176] Ibid.

as a pluralistic but ethnically segregated city."[177] Like other urbanizing cities during the Industrial Revolution and the age of global capitalism, "distinctions between clans, classes, and native or non-native Beirutis remained powerful distinctions within the larger ethnic categories."[178] A clear divide in the city emerged, however, as ethnic tensions rose in the 1950s and 60s. As Calame and Charlesworth write, "a demographic pattern had been established in which the political groups loyal to the Maronite nationalistic platform were concentrated in the eastern side of the city, and those in favor of the predominantly Sunni, pan-Arab platform in the west."[179] East and West Beirut, roughly divided between Christian and Muslim ethnic-religious groups respectively, reflected the power bases of each side during the Lebanese civil war.

The violence of the 1970s in Beirut forced population shifts that led to the city's segregation by religious affiliation. Enclaves of ethnic minorities in Beirut sought security by moving out of the city or moving to areas in which their ethnicity was the majority group. In addition, "about a year after violence first erupted in the city, large-scale coordinated population transfers began in the capital..."[180] This phenomenon is observed in ethnic conflict more generally.[181] For many, this segregated atmosphere was embodied by the Green Line, which served as the de-facto demarcation of

---

[177] Jon Calame, *Divided Cities: Belfast, Beirut, Jerusalem, Mostar, and Nicosia*, City in the Twenty-First Century Book Series (Philadelphia: University of Pennsylvania Press, 2009), 39.

[178] Ibid., 41.

[179] Ibid., 49.

[180] Ibid.

[181] See Stathis N. Kalyvas, "Wanton and Senseless?: The Logic of Massacres in Algeria," *Rationality and Society* 11, no. 3 (1999): 243–85, https://doi.org/10.1177/104346399011003001. Kalyvas, in his study of the logic of massacres, alludes to this phenomenon of group self-segregation: "Massacres will be more likely in areas and periods of declining rebel control; in areas and periods of 'fragmented' rule (when violence can be exercised by both sides); and in an advanced stage of escalation" (p. 251-2). People in fragmented rule, therefore, are most likely to face terrorist attacks. Segregation allows ethnic groups to consolidate control in a specific territory and people who lived in disputed areas added security, thereby resolving the issue of 'fragmented' rule.

East and West Beirut during the civil war.[182] Ethnically-motivated violence that targeted civilians served to reinforce the power of the paramilitary groups as protectors of their religious sect. This caused "the disappearance of mixed residential areas, which were commonplace before the outbreak of hostilities, reduced the chances of reconciliation and accelerated the ethnic polarization of the city."[183] For its part, only a sliver of text in the Taif Accords addresses issues of segregation and displacement, an issue that became a site of contestation after the war.

Post-war reconstruction efforts honed in on a neoliberal vision of peace for Lebanon, focusing on revitalizing Beirut as a financial and leisure center to attract foreign investment and private development. John Nagle identifies the elite's "reconstruction ideology," that is, "…an intentional attempt to erase memories of the war; the process of forgetting conveniently reinforced the nexus between neoliberalism and ethnicity to facilitate the elites' control of economic and political institutions."[184] On the other hand, leaders faced a daunting challenge with the number of internally displaced persons in Lebanon after the civil war. The Ministry for the Displaced and the Central Fund for the Displaced were founded to facilitate property returns. This ministry was headed by Walid Jumblatt, leader of the Progressive Socialist Party and its militia—which alludes to Nagle's point about the motivations behind the political elite's reconstruction philosophy.[185] What transpired was a botched program, rife with "mismanagement and embezzlement of funds."[186] According to Georges Assaf and Rana El-Fil, between 1991 to 1999, $800 million was spent on displacement, but only "20 per cent of the displaced were able to return" and only "nine per cent of those who returned were fully reimbursed

---

[182] E. J. Dionne Jr., "BATTLES PICK UP ON BEIRUT'S GREEN LINE," *The New York Times*, February 27, 1984, https://www.nytimes.com/1984/02/27/world/battles-pick-up-on-beirut-s-green-line.html.

[183] Calame, *Divided Cities*, 54.

[184] John Nagle, "Ghosts, Memory, and the Right to the Divided City: Resisting Amnesia in Beirut City Centre," *Antipode* 49, no. 1 (2017): 149–68, https://doi.org/10.1111/anti.12263, 158.

[185] "Resolving the Issue of War Displacement in Lebanon | Forced Migration Review," accessed February 18, 2021, https://www.fmreview.org/land-and-property-issues/assaf-elfil.

[186] Ibid.

for expenditure on house reconstruction."[187] Clearly, corruption tainted the economic recovery and the return of the displaced, quickly denying Beirut its potential to become a site of coexistence and collaboration.

Put simply, processing displacement claims in Beirut was a mess. An unwieldy bureaucracy and informal patronage networks organized along sectarian affiliation made it close to impossible for displaced persons to claim funds. Aseel Sawalha accounts for the post-war attitude in Beirut, in which segregated spaces became open to all once again, but "they continued to be foreign and unfamiliar to those who lived on 'one side' of the city and who paid cautious visits to the 'other side'."[188] Her ethnographic fieldwork explored the reconstruction efforts in Beirut. She interviewed all those involved in the reconstruction process, from public administrators to displaced person claimants and squatters. Sawalha corroborates Nagle's hypothesis on the post-war reconstruction mindset, as officials believed "the city must be 'cleansed' of all vestiges of the war, and therefore the displaced were mandated to leave the city."[189] But many Lebanese in Beirut, believing that they have a rightful claim for war damages to their homes, fought for their pay-outs. Sawalha interviewed 'Ali' (a pseudonym), a displaced person who filed a claim for his Beirut home. She summed up her encounter succinctly: "Ali's case illustrates how intricately formal systems were interlaced with the informal systems of quid pro quo contracts that evolved directly from wartime practices."[190] What is revealed, in this instance, is a sectarian clientelist framework carried over from the civil war into the government apparatus of a weak state. It is safe to say that the sites of coexistence and collaboration transformed into a contested space in which Beirutis had to go through their sect's patronage channels to get displacement relief. This competition for reparations turned into a zero-sum game between ethnic groups.

The corrupt displacement relief process went hand-in-hand with the rise of Solidere—a pseudo-public-private corporation founded by then prime minister Rafik Hariri in 1994—and its redevelopment of Beirut's

---

[187] Ibid.

[188] Aseel Sawalha, *Reconstructing Beirut: Memory and Space in a Postwar Arab City* (Austin: University of Texas Press, 2010), https://muse.jhu.edu/book/574, 12.

[189] Ibid., 115.

[190] Ibid., 130-1.

city center. Oliver Wainwright speaks of this hybrid oddity, "incorporated as a private business, listed on the stock exchange," but also "[enjoying] special powers of compulsory purchase and regulatory authority" granted by Lebanese law.[191] This gave Solidere extraordinary power to dictate terms favorable for themselves when they bought land in downtown Beirut. Only a handful of wealthy owners, such as Fady el-Khoury (who owns St. George Hotel), have resisted Solidere's encroachment thus far. In building glamourous skyscrapers, waterfront promenades, a yacht club, and luxury shops, the corporation aimed to unify the nation by "deterritorializing space."[192] Once an important "site of social centrality," or a site of coexistence, it has "excluded most of the citizenry" and contributed to the "exacerbation of ethnic cleavages in the postwar era."[193] Areas like the Beirut Souks cater to the highest strata in Lebanese society, excluding the lower class from once shared spaces. Solidere is only one example of the cozy relationship between the political and business elites in Lebanon—the people who sought to rebuild the capital in their own image. When only the rich can intermingle in sites of coexistence, the rest of the Lebanese population are denied the opportunity to interact amongst ethnicities in a meaningful way.

Thirty years after the civil war, residential Beirut remains ethnically divided, although sectarian boundaries are not as rigid as before. Mona Fawaz et al. notes that the boundaries of wartime East and West Beirut "have been weakened but they remain inscribed in the minds of many urbanites, especially when it comes to serious decisions such as choosing a place to dwell."[194] However, neighborhoods are increasingly being differentiated by political alliances, be it March 8 or March 14, where "panoplies of sectarian markers such as flags, emblems, graffiti, and posters are used to demarcate the territory of a group against so-called outsiders

---

[191] "Is Beirut's Glitzy Downtown Redevelopment All That It Seems?," *The Guardian*, January 22, 2015, http://www.theguardian.com/cities/2015/jan/22/beirut-lebanon-glitzy-downtown-redevelopment-gucci-prada.

[192] Nagle, "Ghosts," 155.

[193] Ibid., 159.

[194] Mona Fawaz, Mona Harb, and Ahmad Gharbieh, "Living Beirut's Security Zones: An Investigation of the Modalities and Practice of Urban Security: Living Beirut's Security Zones," *City & Society* 24, no. 2 (August 2012): 173–95, https://doi.org/10.1111/j.1548-744X.2012.01074.x, 181.

and re-affirm the supposed allegiance of insiders."[195] In this case, sectarian allegiances are still salient, with elite-brokered political alliances defining the new in-group, out-group dynamic in Beiruti neighborhoods. This signaling—be it the light blue flags of Saad Hariri's Future Movement or the bright yellow flags of Hezbollah—warns those who may upset the community. Unlike the explicit barriers of the Green Line, these implicit signals harken to civil war control of territory by religious sect.

Figure 10 illustrates the use of posters and political imagery to demarcate ethnic-religious neighborhoods. I took these images during my time in Beirut in 2019. In Photo C, a billboard depicting the Lebanese Forces *(al-Quwwat al-Lubnaniyah)* party symbol and leader Samir Geagea hangs over a building that faces Elias Sarkis Avenue, the main thoroughfare in the East Beirut neighborhood of Achrafieh. This predominantly Maronite Catholic area was once a stronghold for right-wing Christian militias during the war. Up the road, Photo B shows another political billboard, this time of the late Bashir Gemayel. A Lebanese Forces flag can be seen in the foreground. The huge sign is situated in Sassine Square, a main artery in Achrafieh—and directly opposite of the site where Gemayel was assassinated in 1983. Photo A was taken in a Shia Muslim enclave of the Zuqaq el-Blat neighborhood. A young Hezbollah martyr poses with his assault rifle, with the party symbol depicted on the bottom right. These subtle reminders of ethnic belonging emanate in Lebanese society, precisely because of the sites of contestation that politicians have failed to transform.

---

[195] Ibid.

Figure 10. Ethnographic Map of Beirut

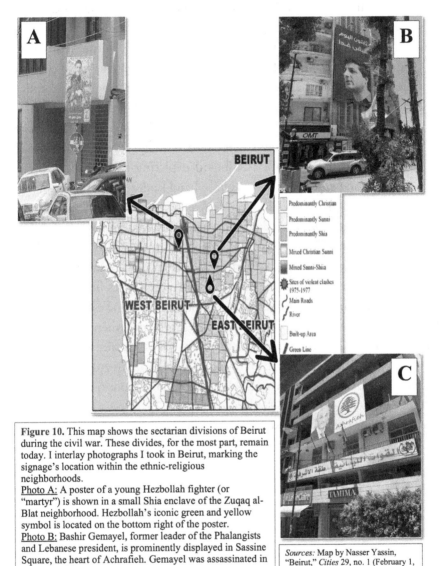

Figure 10. This map shows the sectarian divisions of Beirut during the civil war. These divides, for the most part, remain today. I interlay photographs I took in Beirut, marking the signage's location within the ethnic-religious neighborhoods.

Photo A: A poster of a young Hezbollah fighter (or "martyr") is shown in a small Shia enclave of the Zuqaq al-Blat neighborhood. Hezbollah's iconic green and yellow symbol is located on the bottom right of the poster.

Photo B: Bashir Gemayel, former leader of the Phalangists and Lebanese president, is prominently displayed in Sassine Square, the heart of Achrafieh. Gemayel was assassinated in 1983 near this spot.

Photo C: A Lebanese Forces billboard depicting party leader Samir Geagea hangs in front of Elias Sarkis Avenue in Achrafieh.

Sources: Map by Nasser Yassin, "Beirut," *Cities* 29, no. 1 (February 1, 2012): 69, https://doi.org/10.1016/j.cities.2011.02.001 (Reproduced and adapted with permission from Elsevier). Photographs by Czar Alexei Sepe (June-July 2019).

The intertwined relationship between Beirut's displaced population and economic development after Taif reveals an unpleasant reality behind the hollow words of the power-sharing agreement. By virtue of the sectarian political elites' redevelopment policy, desiring to sanitize the civil war past through leveling parts of the city, a neoliberal outlook on the reconstruction was adopted. Solidere embodied the Lebanese government's emphasis on capitalist growth over the echoes of social justice in the Taif agreement, at the expense of Beirutis who sought financial relief and displacement claims. When public space was monopolized by quasi-public-private corporations like Solidere for the rich, most Lebanese citizens were deprived of a meaningful site of coexistence—most notably, the old Beirut souks. Therefore, the development of Beirut's economic reconstruction, alongside displacement issues, show that due to several factors—political corruption, clientelism, neoliberal governmental policies—the sites of coexistence and collaboration in Taif were not adequately cultivated. Only the rich coexisted and collaborated, in the new Le Yacht Club on the Beirut Marina.

3.8: *Gaging Ethnic Tensions and Sectarian Strife*

Researchers try to gauge ethnic tensions in Lebanon through a systematic, data-driven approach; however, reliable public polling data is hard to come by for the country. To aid my investigation into the extent to which sectarian animosities have increased or decreased since the implementation of the power-sharing regime, I use selected opinion polling from the Arab Barometer and Kenneth Vaughan's logistical regression study. Overall, the data demonstrate that from the end of the civil war to the mid-2010s, ethnic tensions have mostly risen.

The Arab Barometer provides public opinion polling for the MENA (Middle East North Africa) region, including Lebanon. In their "Wave V Country Report," there has been a gradual uptick in the percentage of Lebanese respondents who say they "strongly dislike or dislike having members of a different religion as neighbors": from 2007 to 2010, those who did not wish to live next to other religious sects were 5% but increased to 14% in 2016 and 21% in 2018—a quadrupling in one decade alone.[196] Surprisingly, this differs from the trends in general religious belief in the country. The same report found that "personal piety in Lebanon has declined dramatically in the past decade: only 24 percent [in 2018] describe themselves as religious compared with 44 percent in 2010."[197] Education level does not change the level of piety, as "those with a basic level of education in Lebanon are as likely to be religious as those with a higher degree."[198] These findings suggest that although religiosity is in decline, the essential ethnic identification of religion in Lebanon is still salient—and tension is on the rise.

Kenneth Vaughan investigates the perceptions of democracy between Lebanese ethnic-religious groups to assess the consociational theory in general. His research method uses the Arab Barometer to conduct logistic regression models and assess the relationship between ethnic-religious identity (using the four main ethnic groups: Maronite, Sunni Muslim, Shia Muslim, and Druze) and trust in government institutions.[199] Vaughan reveals that only Shias had consistently favorable views about Lebanon's democracy and government institutions. Compared to Sunni, Maronite, and Druze respondents, "only Shia Muslims rated the Lebanese government as more democratic than undemocratic."[200] The difference between Shia and Maronite views on government institutions is stark: "when it comes to having a general trust in the government and trust in the police, Shia Muslims only have significantly higher odds of trust when compared to Maronite Catholics."[201] For the most part, "evaluations of the freedom that are guaranteed in Lebanon were generally high" for all religious sects, "with the exception of the freedom to sue the government."[202] Vaughan summarizes his statistical analysis research of Lebanon:

---

[196] Lebanon: Country Report – 2019, "Lebanon – Arab Barometer," accessed March 21, 2021, https://www.arabbarometer.org/countries/lebanon/, 16.

[197] Ibid., 15.

[198] Ibid.

[199] Kenneth Vaughan, "Who Benefits from Consociationalism? Religious Disparities in Lebanon's Political System," *Religions* 9, no. 2 (February 2018): 51, https://doi.org/10.3390/rel9020051, 8.

[200] Ibid., 9.

[201] Ibid., 10.

[202] Ibid., 11.

"In ten out of twelve models investigating equal outcomes for the state of democracy, Maronite respondents consistently feel that the state of Lebanon is less democratic, less trustworthy, and less free when compared to Shia Muslims. Similar disparities were observed between Shia and Sunni Muslims in nine out of the twelve models. Similar findings were also found between Shia Muslims and Druze respondents."[203]

According to International Information estimates, the Shia community is now the largest sect in Lebanon. This 2019 independent poll, using unofficial demographic estimates and electoral information from the 2018 parliamentary election, found that Shia represented 31.6% of the population, Sunni 31.1%, and Christians 30.6%.[204] This is the first time since the official 1932 Census that the Shia population has eclipsed all other sectarian groups. In this light, it is likely that the Shia community's high confidence in Lebanese political institutions reflects broader demographic trends in favor of that ethnic group. Their preference and trust in democracy is a function of their claim as the country's majority sect.

Vaughan's investigation raises alarm bells for the state of ethnic relations in Lebanon. Because the faith of political institutions is highly correlated between religious sects, this increases the sectarian animosities in Lebanese society. The Taif Accords diminished the Maronite Catholic community's political power relative to Sunni and Shia power. It appears that as Muslims—especially Shia—grew more powerful both institutionally and demographically, the other religious sects' faith in democracy in Lebanon fell. Coupled with the increased intolerance seen in the Arab Barometer, in the case of living next to those of a different religion, these surveys adequately prove that ethnic tensions have increased in Lebanon since the end of hostilities in the early 1990s. It is interesting to note, however, that the sharp decline in religious belief does not necessarily correlate with a decrease in ethnic tensions. The Arab Barometer report reaffirms the fact

---

[203] Ibid., 13.

[204] "New Report Reveals Substantial Demographic Changes in Lebanon," *annahar.com*, accessed March 21, 2021, https://www.annahar.com/english/article/1002964-new-report-reveals-substantial-demographic-changes-in-lebanon.

that sectarian affiliation in Lebanon is an ethnic identity—not necessarily underpinned by religious faith and conviction.

3.9: *Findings and Conclusions*

Figure 11. Lebanon Case Study Findings

Section of Taif Accords	SSI		Cohesion Strategies		Observed Ethnic Tension
	Predicted	*Observed*	*Predicted*	*Observed*	
Education	Collaboration	Contestation	Assimilation	Not implemented	Increase
Displacement/ General Principles (Economy)	Coexistence	Contestation	Assimilation and Differentiation	Not implemented	Increase

The Taif Accords forged peace for Lebanon, after an acrimonious civil war that devastated the state and its people. It is clear though that the power-sharing agreement was a compromise document, which spliced the divergent interests of the traditional Lebanese political elite, paramilitary leaders and the external power of Syria, into a text rife with contradictions. However, Taif did provide a consociational model that attempted to unify the nation out of the rubble. To sum up, the Taif agreement envisioned education as a space to pursue assimilation (an overarching national identity rooted in Arabness) by creating sites of collaboration, and the economic reconstruction of Beirut as a way to forge sites of coexistence and collaboration (by achieving economic and social justice). Both cases demonstrate that after peace in Lebanon, these provisions in the power-sharing agreements were barely implemented. Rather, the political elite and sectarian groups viewed education and the economy as sites of contestation (a zero-sum game), thereby increasing ethnic tensions. Figure 11 summarizes this chapter's case-study findings.

On balance, the combination of the state's failure to cultivate sites of collaboration and coexistence, and the proliferation of sites of contestation is a causal factor in the increase of ethnic tensions in Lebanon. In this chapter, I establish a causal relationship between the proliferation of sites of contestation and the increase in sectarian animosities in the country after power-sharing was implemented. Due to various socio-political conditions, the proposed sites of collaboration, meant to decrease ethnic tensions, actually became sites of contestation, where ethnic group politics is openly played out and winners and losers are distributed by ethnic belonging. As for the cohesion strategies, due to the agreement's ineffective implementation, the assimilation strategies were not carried through. By in large, an increase in ethnic tensions resulted in the persistent political mobilization on religious lines. Even when the loci of power politics remained sites of contestation, important areas in society that could have led to a furthering of cohesion strategies and sites of social interaction that decreased ethnic tensions *and* were formulated to do so in the Taif accords did not occur. The Taif agreement—if it was truly meant to decrease ethnic salience through a consociational form of democracy—has failed. Thus, I find that the Lebanese case study confirms my hypothesis on the relationship between SSIs, cohesion strategies, ethnic tensions, and power-sharing outcomes.

CHAPTER 4

NORTHERN IRELAND: A FIGHT FOR PEACE

"I will never sit down with Gerry Adams…he'd sit with anyone. He'd sit down with the devil. In fact, Adams does sit down with the devil."

– Rev. Ian Paisley, leader of the Democratic Unionist Party, 1997.[205]

"Up until March 26 this year Ian Paisley and I never had a conversation about anything—not even about the weather."

– Martin McGuinness, leader of Sinn Féin, 2007.[206]

"I always walk with my heart constricting, / Half-expecting bottles, in sudden shards / Of West Belfast sunshine, / To dance about my head."
– Sinéad Morrissey, "Thoughts in a Black Taxi," 1996.[207]

4.1: *Introduction*

In light of the 2016 Brexit referendum, one of the most contentious issues on the negotiating table was Northern Ireland's status in a post-Brexit reality—and how proposed deals may violate the 1998 Belfast

---

[205] "Ian Paisley: 'Never! Never! Never!' And Other Notable Quotes," *The Irish Times*, accessed February 19, 2021, https://www.irishtimes.com/news/politics/ian-paisley-never-never-never-and-other-notable-quotes-1.1926880.

[206] David A. Graham, "The Strange Friendship of Martin McGuinness and Ian Paisley," *The Atlantic*, March 21, 2017, https://www.theatlantic.com/international/archive/2017/03/martin-mcguinness-ian-paisley/520257/.

[207] Sinéad Morrissey, "Thoughts in a Black Taxi," in *There Was Fire In Vancouver* (Manchester, United Kingdom: Carcanet Press Ltd, 1996), 19–20, https://www.proquest.com/docview/2148060035/citation/8559F67403CE4A26PQ/13.

Agreement (Good Friday Agreement).[208] Due to this, as well as the changing demographics in the region, there have been growing calls from nationalists to conduct a border poll referendum on Irish unification in the near future. Nationalists (who are predominantly Catholic and identify as Irish) believe demographic momentum is on their side: the 2011 Census showed only a 3% difference between Protestants (48%) and Catholics (45%), while a more recent poll conducted by the Department of Education showed that from nursery to second-level education, "Catholics make up 50.6 per cent of the schools' population (176,408 pupils) while Protestants make up 32.3 per cent (112,637 pupils)" in the 2019-2020 school year.[209] All sides are awaiting in suspense for the completion of the 2021 Census.[210] But a border poll, triggered through the mechanisms outlined in the Northern Irish power-sharing agreement, risks stirring up sectarian animosities and re-surfacing the violence of the not-so-distant past.

There is a precarious peace in Northern Ireland. Since the adoption of the 1998 Northern Ireland Act, establishing the devolved Northern Irish government, power-sharing has collapsed five times. This includes two long durations without a government in recent history (2002-2007 and 2017-2020).[211] A power-sharing deal was struck in January 2020, only after the two main political parties—the Democratic Unionist Party (DUP) and

---

[208] See Jonathan Tonge, "The Impact and Consequences of Brexit for Northern Ireland," *European Parliament,* https://www.europarl.europa.eu/RegData/etudes/BRIE/2017/583116/IPOL_BRI%282017%29583116_EN.pdf; "Brexit Is Just Weeks Old, and It's Already Threatening Fragile Political Stability in Northern Ireland," *CNN,* accessed February 22, 2021, https://www.cnn.com/2021/02/06/uk/brexit-northern-ireland-violence-threat-intl/index.html. for the lively debate on this issue, which is very much in play as of the writing of this chapter (March 2021).

[209] Gerry Moriarty, "Northern Ireland: Polls Can Provide More Confusion than Clarity," *The Irish Times,* accessed February 22, 2021, https://www.irishtimes.com/news/ireland/irish-news/northern-ireland-polls-can-provide-more-confusion-than-clarity-1.4344768.

[210] Charlie Bradley, "Census 2021 Warning as Survey Could Lead to UK Split: 'Referendum Will Happen!,'" *Express.co.uk,* March 20, 2021, https://www.express.co.uk/news/uk/1412629/census-2021-news-survey-uk-northern-ireland-referendum-brexit-deadline-spt.

[211] "Summary: Governing without Ministers," *The Institute for Government,* September 25, 2019, https://www.instituteforgovernment.org.uk/summary-governing-without-ministers-northern-ireland.

Sinn Féin (SF)—performed poorly in the 2019 General Election, and the UK Government threatened another round of elections for the region.[212] Ethnic tensions are persistent. From 'peace walls' that separate ethnic-religious communities to the annual parade season, in which (mostly) Protestant groups march to commemorate loyalist historical milestones, sectarian animosity remains a tough hurdle in cross-community reconciliation. Nevertheless, there have been inroads in the peace process, and ethnic violence in Northern Ireland has decreased drastically. Pat Nolan found that "158 'security-related' deaths" have occurred in the twenty years since the GFA, which pales in comparison to the 480 deaths that occurred in 1972—in one year *alone*—at the peak of the Troubles.[213] Part of the compromise settlement that brought back power-sharing in 2020 recognizes both Irish and Ulster Scots as official languages in the country.[214] Certainly, progress has been made to ameliorate ethnic tensions in Northern Ireland, but to what extent did the Good Friday Agreement affect ethnic tensions in the region?

This chapter will explore the role of the Good Friday Agreement in establishing power-sharing institutions and sites of social interaction conducive to decreasing ethnic tensions in Northern Ireland. Unlike Lebanon, Northern Ireland did not have historical roots in power-sharing. Northern Ireland was formed to preserve a Protestant-majority polity on the island of Ireland. But Protestant dominance could not last. By 1968, violence erupted in the cities of (London-) Derry and Belfast, commencing the Troubles. Throughout this ethnic conflict, efforts were made—although unsuccessfully—to reach some form of political settlement via consociationalism. This led to the Belfast Agreement in 1998. Although it proved to be a challenge to implement, the power-sharing agreement fared well—as it was fully implemented in a decade.

I then embark on a textual analysis of the Good Friday Agreement. The

---

[212] "The Northern Ireland Peace Process," *Council on Foreign Relations*, accessed February 22, 2021, https://www.cfr.org/backgrounder/northern-ireland-peace-process.

[213] "'158 Security-Related Deaths' since Good Friday Agreement," *BBC News*, accessed February 22, 2021, https://www.bbc.com/news/uk-northern-ireland-43862294.

[214] "A Breakthrough for Language Rights in Northern Ireland," *OHRH*, February 18, 2020, https://ohrh.law.ox.ac.uk/a-breakthrough-for-language-rights-in-northern-ireland/.

power-sharing arrangement, which encompassed a plethora of issues, had overall SSIs of coexistence and collaboration, and a differentiation cohesion strategy. To better understand the GFA's implementation and whether my predictions correspond to actual outcomes, I process trace two aspects of the agreement: anti-discrimination and employment and decommissioning of paramilitary groups. Both cases demonstrate success in implementing the envisioned sites of social interaction, as well as the overall cohesion strategies. The case of decommissioning shows the fluid progression of SSIs throughout the implementation process, as I find that it was a site of contestation at first, but then transitioned to a site of coexistence. Through my analysis of public opinion polling, I conclude that there has been a slight decrease in ethnic tensions. Thus, my hypotheses are congruent with the Northern Irish case study, thereby amplifying its explanatory power.

4.2: *A History of Northern Ireland, Sans Power-Sharing*

To explain the origins of the Northern Irish conflict, we must situate any historical analysis in the greater context of the English conquest of Ireland—most importantly, the Ulster Plantations in the seventeenth century. Under Queen Elizabeth I's reign, the traditional Irish province of Ulster (comprised of nine counties: Antrim, Armagh, Cavan, Donegal, Down, Fermanagh, Londonderry/Derry, Monaghan, and Tyrone) were subdued by English forces after the defeat of the native Irish chieftains. The Crown confiscated land as the Irish nobility fled. In turn, subsequent British monarchs consolidated their hold on the island by distributing the land to colonists arriving from Britain.[215] This colonial enterprise was accelerated by Oliver Cromwell during the English Civil War. His New Model Army ruthlessly conquered a resistant native population

---

[215] "CAIN: Conflict in Northern Ireland: A Background Essay," accessed February 24, 2021, https://cain.ulster.ac.uk/othelem/facets.htm#chap2.

and raised Catholic towns, like Drogheda, in 1649.[216] By the 1700s, the plantations were viewed as a success. As John Darby writes: "by 1703, less than 5 per cent of the land of Ulster was still in the hands of the Catholic Irish."[217] Colonists came from the British isle, many of whom were Scottish, and established settlements while they pushed out native Irish onto undesirable land in the west. Sectarian dividing lines emerged rather quickly because most colonists were Protestant while most natives were Catholics. Furthermore, a system of Penal Codes in the 1700s prevented Irish Catholics from "bearing arms, educating their children and owning any horse above £5 in value," while Protestants affiliated with the Church of Ireland—both north and south—enjoyed landownership and self-rule during a period called the Protestant Ascendancy. Over time, these defining characteristics, including a sense of discrimination and deprivation, would form divergent ethnic identities that will come into confrontation in the nineteenth and twentieth centuries. It is no surprise, as John Coakley holds, that "religious background has been the most fundamental determinant of national identity in Northern Ireland."[218]

Similar to the Lebanese state, the creation of Northern Ireland as a distinct political entity was a recent invention—dating to the Government of Ireland Act 1920 (and six years before *Grand Liban*). At the heart of this new 'Northern' Island lies competing political claims over self-determination: on one hand, Irish nationalists demanded that Northern Ireland be absorbed into the Irish state; on the other, unionists demanded that the territory remain a separate political entity under the 'union' of

---

[216] See Henry Tichborne, *A Letter of Sir Henry Tichborne to His Lady, of the Siege of Drogheda; and Other Passages of the Wars of Ireland Where He Commanded.*, Eighteenth Century; Reel 11081, No. 14 (Drogheda: printed by John Fleming, 1772). This primary document is a first-hand account to the siege of Drogheda, and the subsequent massacre of the native Irish in the town. Historical events like these serve as reminders of British repression for Northern Irish nationalists and republicans, to this day.

[217] "CAIN: Conflict in Northern Ireland: A Background Essay."

[218] John Coakley, "National Identity in Northern Ireland: Stability or Change?," *Nations and Nationalism* 13, no. 4 (2007): 573–97, https://doi.org/10.1111/j.1469-8129.2007.00316.x, 577.

the United Kingdom.[219] Therefore, the key to understanding the country's history and ethnic conflict is the inherent interests of the two external powers involved in each side's claims—the newly independent Irish Free State (Ireland) and Great Britain (UK). Whether 'nationalist' or 'unionist,' a closer history that traces the reasons why Northern Ireland was partitioned by the UK will inform us about the country's ethnic-religious group dynamic.

In many respects, the Northern Irish government was meant to be a solution against competing Irish nationalist and Ulster unionist aspirations within Great Britain. This competition was exemplified in the Home Rule crises. As Irish cultural and political nationalism predicated on a Catholic, Gaelic identity came into full swing during the nineteenth and early twentieth century (the Gaelic Revival), a parallel reaction against this conceptualization of the Irish nation took hold amongst the traditionally Protestant Ulster-Scots in the north. After two failed attempts to form a local governing body, known as Home Rule, the Third Home Rule Bill introduced in 1912 was on the verge of passing in Westminster.[220] Fearful of a Catholic-majority government, unionists coalesced under the Ulster Volunteer Force, a paramilitary group, and swore a solemn oath and covenant with over 500,000 like-minded Irish to "[use] all means which may be found necessary to defeat" Home Rule.[221] This mass-mobilization alarmed Westminster, as British Liberals and Conservatives alike viewed "partition as a solution" to the Irish question.[222]

Meanwhile, republican nationalists in the south steadily built up their own paramilitary groups and rebelled against Great Britain in the 1916 Easter Rising. This rebellion, though squashed in a week by British forces, marked the beginning of Ireland's independence era. Many Irish resorted to arms in a nationalist struggle to declare Ireland a republic, free from

---

[219] John McGarry, *Explaining Northern Ireland: Broken Images* (Oxford ; Cambridge, Mass.: Blackwell, 1995), 35-6.

[220] Jonathan Bardon, *A History of Ulster*, New updated ed. (Belfast, Northern Ireland: Blackstaff Press, 2001), 431.

[221] "About the Ulster Covenant," *nidirect*, December 1, 2015, https://www.nidirect. gov.uk/articles/about-ulster-covenant; *Ulster's Solemn League and Covenant : Being Convinced in Our Consciences That Home Rule Would Be Disastrous to the Material Well-Being of Ulster as Well as of the Whole of Ireland... /* (s.n., 1912).

[222] Bardon, 446.

the British monarchy. Fighting intensified in the south between 1919 and 1920, as the Irish Republican Army (IRA), led by Michael Collins, employed guerilla tactics to subvert the heavy British military presence. On the political front, the 1920 Government of Ireland Act implemented Home Rule, which was originally delayed because of the First World War. In accordance with the law, two parliaments—one for twenty-six southern counties and the other for six counties in Ulster (Antrim, Armagh, Down, Fermanagh, Londonderry/Derry, and Tyrone)—were created.[223] Nevertheless, republican guerillas continued to fight British forces until the 1921 Anglo-Irish Treaty, which created the Irish Free State, a political entity with a looser relationship between the Crown and southern Ireland. After a short, but bloody, civil war between those who accepted the treaty and those who opposed it, the fledgling Irish Free State entered the 1925 London Agreement, which "abandoned both the nationalists in the North and the hope for all-Ireland unity."[224] In short, Northern Ireland was created to maintain a Protestant-majority polity—concentrated in six northern counties—loyal to Great Britain on the island, despite the independence-seeking Catholic majority in Ireland.

Ulster unionists ceaselessly consolidated their power in the newly-formed Northern Ireland parliament, introducing legislation to essentially crystallize their rule in the country. The Ulster Special Constabulary was established by the end of 1920, in response to a "'feeling of insecurity' in Belfast."[225] However, as Thomas Hennessey notes, "the force that emerged was based mainly on a reorganized UVF and therefore almost exclusively Protestant," thereby making justice and policing solely the domain of the ethnic majority.[226] The creation of an independent state in southern Ireland, in 1937, polarized Ulster along sectarian lines, as bouts of ethnic violence erupted in urban centers such as Derry (Londonderry).[227] Jonathan Bardon points out the immense challenge a new Northern Irish government faced:

---

[223] Roger H. Hull, *The Irish Triangle: Conflict in Northern Ireland*, Princeton Legacy Library (Princeton, New Jersey; Guildford, England: Princeton University Press, 1976), 19-20.

[224] Ibid., 36.

[225] Thomas Hennessey, *A History of Northern Ireland, 1920-1996* (Dublin: Gill & Macmillan, 1997), 15.

[226] Ibid.

[227] Bardon, 494-6.

"the fact that a third of the population was so hostile to the six-county state that it hoped for its downfall would have taxed the ingenuity of any government of the region."[228] For their part, northern unionists felt isolated as a minority in the whole of the island, so they entrenched themselves into the Northern Irish political apparatus. As violence spiraled out of control, the Northern Irish government took drastic measures, enacting the Civil Authority (Special Powers) Act in 1922, which "amounted to the civil equivalent of the statutory imposition of martial law."[229] These draconian measures foreshadow the extent to which the new country would go to protect its majority-Protestant status.

Unlike the history of Lebanon, where the spirit of power-sharing comes from a legacy that dates back to Ottoman rulers and was encoded in the nation's founding, Northern Ireland's politicians sought to maintain one-party rule throughout the early to mid-twentieth century. Proportional representation was abolished in 1923, and soon after, "Unionist representation on elected public bodies increased at the expense of all other parties."[230] Sir James Craig sought a "clear-cut division between loyalism and nationalism."[231] It was effective: "there had been only eight uncontested seats in 1925 but by 1933 there were thirty-three—70 per cent."[232] This, alongside a 1924 electoral commission that gerrymandered the boundaries of local government, solidified Protestant, Unionist rule. Catholic, nationalist communities did not contest these changes out of protest, but this tactic damaged their cause in the long run, as Paul Bew argues.[233] In local Northern Irish councils, the property valuation system, whereby the local franchise was granted to men who met property qualifications, disproportionately represented Unionists. Nationalists claimed this discriminated against them, but it was standard practice to use this system both in Britain and Ireland.[234] These actions carried significant political weight in favor of Protestant Unionists, but also demonstrate a

---

[228] Ibid., 496.

[229] Hennessey, 33.

[230] Ibid., 45.

[231] Ibid., 98.

[232] Bardon, 511.

[233] Paul Bew, *Northern Ireland 1921-1994: Political Forces and Social Classes* (London: Serif, 1995), 48.

[234] Hennessey, 52.

"vicious circle of distrust" as "the question of discrimination was coloured as much by the preconceived notions of Nationalists as by the actions of Unionists"—a cycle that will evolve and perpetuate as the seeds of ethnic political conflict were sown.[235]

In the south, the newly-elected Taoiseach (prime minister) Éamon de Valera rewrote the constitution to distance Ireland's relationship with Britain. The brainchild of de Valera, the 1937 *Bunreacht na hÉireann* (Irish Constitution) institutionalized Irish republican ideology in relation to Northern Ireland, posing territorial claims in Articles 2 and 3. For instance, the original Article 2 stated: "the national territory consists of the *whole* island of Ireland, its island and the territorial seas [emphasis added]."[236] Thus, the new state of *Éire* (Ireland) claimed legitimate sovereignty over Northern Ireland. For the Stormont government, this constitutional irredentist claim confirmed their distrust of the Catholic community. This beleaguered mentality, in which Protestants were a majority in Northern Ireland but a minority on the island of Ireland, carried an immense ideological sway for years to come.

The British government took a hands-off approach in Northern Ireland, which gave Unionists an opportunity to build a Protestant state through the civil service and economic reforms. Although many republican and Marxist interpretations of the Northern Irish conflict posit that Unionist dominance was actively created by Westminster, McGarry contends that "control actually established by the Ulster Unionist Party between 1920 and 1972 was not planned, but rather was sanctioned by the neglect of successive British governments."[237] For example, the newly-established Northern Ireland Civil Service (NICS) was intended to be run efficiently, like other imperial bureaucracies in the British empire. Nevertheless, "instances of discrimination against well qualified Catholics occurred from the very beginning" and nationalists were excluded from civil service appointment boards.[238] In the economic sphere, Northern Ireland suffered from stagnation because of the changing global market after the First

---

[235] Ibid., 52-3.
[236] "Bunreacht Na HÉireann (Constitution of Ireland)," accessed March 1, 2021, https://celt.ucc.ie/published/E900003-005/text002.html, 4.
[237] McGarry, *Explaining Northern Ireland*, 45.
[238] Bew, 57.

World War. This made its traditional Northern Irish industries, like linen and shipbuilding, uncompetitive. To respond to this economic decline, the government apparatus adopted a "step-by-step" policy, in which Northern Ireland's welfare state would mirror British social services, including health insurance and unemployment benefits.[239]

It is apparent that Northern Ireland did not have a historical tradition of consociational power-sharing, unlike Lebanon. The partition of the northern counties produced a Protestant-majority political entity that wished to remain in the United Kingdom. The country's early years reveal that power-sharing was not on the table, at least for the unionist politicians. Most of the Catholic minority believed that the Northern Irish state was illegitimate, while most Protestants saw Catholic opposition towards the Stormont government as a confirmation of their worst fears: that a sizeable minority in the region would pose an existential threat to Northern Ireland. British negligence, coupled with Irish irredentism, allowed Ulster unionists to maintain ethnic-majority rule until conditions made it untenable in the 1960s. In hindsight, the historical development of Northern Ireland demonstrates why any conflict resolution—power-sharing or otherwise—must also involve the Republic of Ireland and the United Kingdom. Unfortunately, the negotiating parties came to this realization only after decades of sectarian turmoil.

4.3: *Outbreak of the Troubles and the Seeds of Power-Sharing*

The Irish historian Tim Pat Coogan paints a familiar picture in his account of the Troubles' origins. He notes how the Catholic minority's rise in education levels after the Second World War, their subsequent awareness of their relative economic deprivation, and the transnational civil rights movements of the 1960s coalesced to provide the ingredients for the 'powder keg' of civil unrest.[240] The issue of housing was the spark that lit up ethnic relations. The Northern Ireland Civil Rights Association (NICRA), "a broad-based civil rights movement," demanded significant reforms from

---

[239] Ibid.

[240] Tim Pat Coogan, *The Troubles: Ireland's Ordeal 1966-1996 and the Search for Peace* (Boulder, Colo.: Roberts Rinehart Publishers, 1997), 26-32.

the Ulster Unionist Party (UUP) government. Their manifesto expressed policy proposals to uplift the Catholic minority's standing in society: "a call for 'one man, one vote'," an "end to discrimination and gerrymandering," and "fair play in public housing allocation," among others.[241] They employed civil disobedience tactics that mirrored the US Civil Rights movement—even singing *We Shall Overcome* in demonstrations in (London-) Derry.[242] However, the hope and optimism were squashed. The Royal Ulster Constabulary (RUC), Northern Ireland's police force, violently attacked NICRA protestors in October 1968. Riots and burnings consumed predominantly Catholic areas like Falls Road in Belfast in August 1969, as certain 'B-Specials' patrols protected Protestant, loyalist mobs.[243] As prime minister Terence O'Neill failed to control the situation and did little to appease an aggrieved Catholic population, riled-up by a perception of deep injustice in the country's institutions, Northern Ireland descended into a period of political violence and terrorism.

Figure 12. Political and Military Actors during the Troubles (1968-1998)

Ethnic-Religious Group	Catholic		Protestant	
Political Ideology	Republicanism: violent means to achieve Irish unity	Nationalism: constitutional means to achieve Irish unity	Unionism: constitutional means to maintain union with UK	Loyalism: violent means to maintain union with UK

Figure 12 provides a simple breakdown of the four key political groups that emerged amidst the outbreak of violence. Nationalists, who were mostly Catholic, believed in uniting Northern Ireland with the Republic of Ireland in the south through political means; Republicans, who were

---

[241] Ibid., 56-7.

[242] Ibid., 60.

[243] Ibid., 89-91.

also nationalists, supported an armed struggle to achieve this end.[244] Unionists, who were mostly Protestant, believed in the political union with the UK and opposed Irish unification; Loyalists, who were unionists, supported an armed defense of the union.[245] It is important to stress that although each religious community is not purely monolithic in its political stance vis-à-vis nationalism and unionism, one's sectarian ethnic group is a primary political identifier in Northern Ireland, especially during the Troubles. Similar to the Lebanese civil war dynamic, different factions vie for political control within ethnic communities in Northern Ireland. As the conflict intensified into the 1970s, religious-ethnic polarization and mistrust between communities pushed nationalist and unionist political demands further into the extremes of republicanism and loyalism.

As early as the 1970s, British and Irish leaders sought a political solution to the ethnic conflict that would placate nationalist and unionist interests. The 1973 Sunningdale Agreement marked a milestone in British-Irish relations, as it "was the first occasion since 1925 that the Prime Minister of the United Kingdom, the Taoiseach (Irish Prime Minister), and the Northern Ireland government…had attended the same talks on the future of Northern Ireland."[246] This marked a recognition that any power-sharing solution in Northern Ireland must include considerations from the UK and Ireland. Sunningdale was short-lived, however. The Ulster Workers Council (UWC) and loyalist paramilitary groups mobilized anti-agreement Unionists to hold a general strike and put Northern Ireland at a standstill. The Northern Ireland Executive collapsed, only five months after the settlement—and peace was deferred.

In 1985, the Anglo-Irish Agreement (AIA) made strides in forging power-sharing frameworks that reflected the Catholic, nationalist desire for greater political representation in Northern Ireland. The main breakthrough of this agreement was that it clearly acknowledged the Irish dimension of the Troubles, thereby "placing the conflict in its proper

---

[244] "Northern Ireland Political Parties | Special Reports," *The Guardian*, accessed March 1, 2021, https://www.theguardian.com/politics/northernirelandassembly/page/0,,1090664,00.html.

[245] Ibid.

[246] "CAIN: Events: The Sunningdale Agreement - Chronology of Main Events," accessed February 24, 2021, https://cain.ulster.ac.uk/events/sunningdale/chron.htm.

British-Irish context."[247] In a sense, the conflict was internationalized. McGarry and O'Leary comment on the treaty's important step "as an attempt to create the conditions for power-sharing to work, as a master-plan to coerce key factions of the unionist bloc to accept some version of the 1973-4 settlement [Sunningdale] as the least of several evils."[248] P.J. McLoughlin highlights political shifts in the Catholic community because the AIA "may have encouraged a rethink within republicanism" and the value of engaging with the British state politically.[249] Though the AIA ultimately failed to secure peace, it did ameliorate British-Irish relations in regard to Northern Ireland and paved the way for the multi-dimensional aspect of the Belfast Agreement.

The 1993 Downing Street Declaration (DSD) was the last intermediary step for all parties, including paramilitary groups, to achieve the Good Friday Agreement five years later. Like the AIA, the Downing Street Declaration was an intergovernmental agreement that affirmed the principle of consent for issues pertaining to the future constitution of Northern Ireland. As Sinn Féin and the Provisional IRA shifted their stance on the use of political violence in the mid-1980s and early 1990s, both the British and Irish governments hoped to integrate republicanism into the mainstream, "to persuade republicans to abandon violence whilst not completely alienating mainstream unionism," as Eamonn O'Kane contends.[250] This was no easy feat. Plenty of moving parts, involving dialogues between the Catholic community (the Humes-Adams talks) and Dublin and Westminster culminated in this statement that sets the preconditions for the GFA. The United States put external pressure on all parties to find a political solution. Hence, the DSD was the penultimate

---

[247] Paul Arthur, "Northern Ireland," in *A Concise Oxford Dictionary of Politics and International Relations* (Oxford University Press, 2018), https://www.oxfordreference.com/view/10.1093/acref/9780199670840.001.0001/acref-9780199670840-e-916.

[248] McGarry, *The Northern Ireland Conflict*, 73.

[249] P. J. McLoughlin, "'The First Major Step in the Peace Process'? Exploring the Impact of the Anglo-Irish Agreement on Irish Republican Thinking," *Irish Political Studies* 29, no. 1 (January 2, 2014): 116–33, https://doi.org/10.1080/07907184.2013.875895, 130.

[250] Eamonn O'Kane, "Anglo–Irish Relations and the Northern Ireland Peace Process: From Exclusion to Inclusion," *Contemporary British History* 18, no. 1 (March 1, 2004): 78–99, https://doi.org/10.1080/1361946042000217310, 97.

episode in the resolution of the Troubles. In fact, the IRA would call a cease-fire eight months after the DSD on August 31, 1994, followed by the loyalist paramilitaries in October—setting the stage for peace.

4.4: *The Good Friday Agreement and the 'Parity of Esteem'*

The Belfast Agreement—signed on Good Friday, April 10, 1998—was a multi-faceted power-sharing agreement and peace settlement, involving the UK, the Republic of Ireland, and all parties in Northern Ireland, including paramilitary groups. It was lauded as a political solution to the ethnic conflict that consumed Northern Ireland for thirty years. The culmination of arduous negotiations, the power-sharing agreement encapsulated a whole plethora of issues, ranging from electoral formulas to human rights. This complex treaty encompassed the British isles, in three so-called 'Strands': the internal affairs of Northern Ireland, North-South Ireland relations, and British-Irish relations. With the GFA's sheer breadth, I will provide a brief overview of the text by highlighting specific sections that are pertinent to my investigation of power-sharing and ethnic tensions.

Heading into the final negotiations, UK prime minister Tony Blair identified two principles for a deal; namely, "constitutional reassurances for Unionists" and "equality for Nationalists in Northern Ireland."[251] What underpins the multilateral agreement is the principle of 'parity of esteem.' Jyrki Ruohomaki describes parity of esteem as a normative concept "grounded in the assumption that there are two mutually exclusive and hostile political cultures in Northern Ireland, and that those cultures must be accommodated."[252] Through this pragmatic, and perhaps pessimistic notion, parity of esteem is a basis for coexistence between both communities in Northern Ireland. Further, the GFA is not only an internal peace settlement but also an international treaty between Ireland and the UK. This means that in the sections addressing Irish and UK relations,

---

[251] See Thomas Hennessey, *The Northern Ireland Peace Process: Ending the Troubles?* (Dublin: Gill & Macmillan, 2000) for more insight on the referenda process.

[252] Jyrki Ruohomaki, "Parity of Esteem: A Conceptual Approach to the Northern Ireland Conflict," *Alternatives: Global, Local, Political* 35, no. 2 (April 1, 2010): 163–86, 164.

there is no cohesion strategy for Northern Ireland because it deals with international issues and not the cohesion of an internally fragmented society. Figure 13 provides a breakdown of the Belfast Agreement, according to my frameworks.

Figure 13. Sites of Social Interaction (SSIs) and Cohesion Strategies in the GFA

Section of The GFA	Site(s) of Social Interaction	Cohesion Strategy	Summary of textual analysis
Strand One	Contestation	Assimilation and Differentiation	Institutional mechanisms and electoral procedures temper winners and shelter losers. Major decisions made with cross-community support. Group identity designations in parliament enshrine ethnic power-sharing.
Strand Two	Collaboration	N/A	Greater cooperation between N. and S. Ireland, including suggestions for spheres of cooperation and coordination between governments.
Strand Three	Collaboration	N/A	Institutional forums designed to exchange information and coordinate issues of shared interest: UK and Irish governments, and nations of the British isles.

Human Rights and Equality	Coexistence and Collaboration	Assimilation and Differentiation	Human rights language and calls for anti-discrimination legislation. Enshrines the concept of 'parity of esteem' in cultural spheres like language and symbols.
Justice and Policing	Collaboration	Differentiation	Overhaul of the criminal justice system, community confidence in the police, provides a timeline for decommissioning.
Overall Agreement	Coexistence and Collaboration	Differentiation	'Parity of esteem' as the overarching principle to promote tolerance in Northern Ireland, with efforts to promote cross-community and cross-country dialogue and interaction.

In Strand One, consociation and power-sharing theories guide the structure of devolved government in Northern Ireland. Section 4 states that "The Assembly – operating on a cross-community basis – will be the prime source of authority in respect of all devolved responsibilities."[253] Under "Safeguards," institutional mechanisms to ensure consociational decision-making are outlined, plus the proportional allocation of Committee memberships and Ministers, "parallel consent" of a majority of unionists and nationalists, a "weighted majority" of 60% of members on important decisions like the budget, and an "Equality Commission" to monitor equal rights violations between communities in public bodies.[254] Thus, all major political decisions must be made by a national supermajority, binding together unionist and nationalist decision-making via a strategy of assimilation. Members elected to the Assembly must declare an

---

[253] "Northern Ireland Peace Agreement (The Good Friday Agreement) | UN Peacemaker," accessed October 14, 2020, https://peacemaker.un.org/uk-ireland-good-friday98., 7.

[254] Ibid.

affiliation: unionist, nationalist, or other.[255] This is in line with a strategy of differentiation. An Executive, discharged by a jointly-elected First and Deputy First Minister, would lead an Executive Committee with its seats allocated to political parties through the d'Hondt system.[256] Although unwieldy and complicated, the institutional make-up of the Northern Irish government forces cross-community cooperation on major issues. The country's consociational, power-sharing disposition is affirmed through its implementation of affiliation reporting in the Northern Ireland Assembly. In this vein, Strand One envisions a site of contestation that is dampened by collaborative measures, mitigating the winner-loser dynamic inherent in sites of contestation. It also proscribes a strategy of assimilation and differentiation.

Strand Two underscores the unique relationship between northern and southern Ireland, creating the North/South Ministerial Council (NSMC) as a compromise between nationalist aspirations and unionist concerns. In essence, the cross-island Council aims to "bring together those with executive responsibilities in Northern Ireland and the Irish Government, to develop consultation, co-operation and action within the island of Ireland…on matters of mutual interest within the competence of the Administrations, North and South."[257] This compromise allows for the greater cooperation between north and south desired by nationalists while assuaging unionist fears that the NSMC would be a skeletal framework for a united Irish government, by explicitly deriving its authority through each country's legislative assembly. The Annex of Strand Two suggests twelve areas of cooperation, such as agriculture, education, tourism, and transport.[258] This section provides for a site of collaboration, a forum for which mutual interest between north and south could be discussed and acted upon. Because the enactment of NSMC policies is contingent on both legislatures, Council decisions must be made with a broad consensus

---

[255] Ibid., 8.

[256] Ibid., 8-9. See Silvia Kotandis, "Understanding the d'Hondt Method," *European Parliamentary Research Service*, https://www.europarl.europa.eu/RegData/etudes/BRIE/2019/637966/EPRS_BRI(2019)637966_EN.pdf, for more information about the d'Hondt method of allocating parliamentary seats. This system was already used by the newly-established European Parliament.

[257] "Northern Ireland Peace Agreement," 13.

[258] Ibid., 15.

in north and south Ireland. Ultimately, Strand Two particularly caters to Northern Ireland's Catholic, nationalist communities, who seek a closer relationship with the Republic of Ireland.

To wrap up the agreement, Strand Three addresses British-Irish relations, establishing the British-Irish Council (BIC) and the British-Irish Intergovernmental Conference (BIIC) to allay unionist discomfort over Northern Ireland's closer relationship to the Republic in the previous section. The goal of the BIC is to "promote the harmonious and mutually beneficial development of the totality of relationships among the peoples of these islands," and thus creating an institutional forum for all nations in the British isles.[259] Through consensus decision-making, the BIC would deliberate on "common policies or common actions."[260] Another intergovernmental institution, the BIIC, would "bring together the British and Irish Governments to promote bilateral co-operation at all levels on all matters of mutual interest" through a standing intergovernmental forum.[261] This section addresses how the British and Irish governments would consult each other on "issues of mutual concern in relation to Northern Ireland," institutionalizing the dual relationship of the region and solidifying the two government's shared interest in maintaining peace and governance. The Third Strand interlocks two sites of collaboration, between the constituent nations of the British isles and between the sovereign governments of the UK and the Republic of Ireland. Nonetheless, these sites scantily arise because of the high bar of consensus needed to enact policy. Implicit in these institutions is the acknowledgment of Northern Ireland's close ties to the Union, conceding institutional support for unionists via isle-wide political bodies.

Further areas addressed in the Agreement are human rights and equality, economic, social, and cultural issues. This distinguishes the Belfast Agreement from Taif, as its breadth of topics for consideration demonstrates how truly encompassing this treaty was. Of course, it is one thing to write all these provisions down on paper, and another to enact them. The GFA reaffirms human rights, and a "commitment to the mutual respect, the civil rights and the religious liberties of everyone in the

---

[259] Ibid., 16.

[260] Ibid.

[261] Ibid., 17.

community."[262] This section calls for the creation of a Northern Ireland Human Rights Commission and Equality Commission to safeguard human rights and equality throughout society.[263] Moreover, the agreement "recognizes that victims have a right to remember as well as to contribute to a changed society," as it states the "essential aspect of the reconciliation process," which is "the promotion of a culture of tolerance at every level of society..."[264] With respect to economic and cultural spheres, this section acknowledges the need to address the "differential in unemployment rates between the two communities" and the importance of "linguistic diversity" in Northern Ireland.[265] Many bold pronouncements on human rights and equality make this section quite progressive—but also ambiguous. These areas, once intense sites of contestation during the Troubles, are envisioned as sites of coexistence and collaboration. Assimilation and differentiation are both pursued, implying that all will benefit economically as one unit, while culture will be respected by both communities. 'Mutual respect' keeps appearing in the text and is indicative of this coexistence and collaborative lens.

The last provisions of the GFA covering justice, policing, and the decommissioning of paramilitaries became the most contentious. A stated goal of the agreement is to "achieve the decommissioning of all paramilitary arms within two years following endorsement...of the agreement," a timeline that was too slow for unionists, and too fast for nationalists.[266] For policing and justice, the document stresses that there must be "a new beginning to policing in Northern Ireland with police services capable of attracting and sustaining support from the community as a whole."[267] It adds certain aims in the creation of a new criminal justice system:

> "deliver a fair and impartial system of justice to the community; be responsive to the community's concerns, and encouraging community involvement

---

[262] Ibid., 18.

[263] Ibid., 19-20.

[264] Ibid., 20.

[265] Ibid., 20-1.

[266] Ibid., 22.

[267] Ibid., 23.

where appropriate; have the confidence of all parts of the community; and deliver justice efficiently and effectively."[268]

A Commission on Policing for Northern Ireland and a Review of the Criminal Justice System are sketched out in subsequent sections, presenting the parameters for which public bodies can determine new legislation, regulations, and policy moving forward. These issues divided the Protestant and Catholic communities and would be a sticking point in the initial implementation of the Belfast Agreement. Like other hotly-contested spheres of social interaction during the Troubles, policing and decommissioning proved to be sites of contestation. In this case, the agreement attempts to transform these institutions to become sites of collaboration—a drastic move, considering the intense political violence and terrorism that both communities viewed as legitimizing the use of force, whether from the Royal Ulster Constabulary, the British Army, the IRA, or loyalist paramilitaries.

Figure 14. Northern Ireland Predicted Outcomes

Overall Agreement	Coexistence and Collaboration	Differentiation	Hypotheses
Predicted Ethnic Tensions	Increase/ Decrease and Decrease	Increase/ Decrease	On balance, more factors indicate a likely decrease rather than increase in ethnic tension
Predicted Power-Sharing Outcome	Limited Failure/ Limited Success and Success	Limited Failure/ Limited Success	On balance, more factors indicate power-sharing limited success than limited failure.

---

[268] Ibid.

Similar to the Taif Agreement, the GFA resorted to "constructive ambiguity" in the text so the multiple parties could agree to its ratification.[269] This gave the various parties room for maneuvering, because they could interpret the open-ended parts of the agreement, and its specificities, in a way that would garner support from their divergent communities. Nonetheless, the power-sharing agreement, as Arthur Aughey suggests, was meant to be transformative: "The reconstitution of Northern Ireland had become the deconstruction of Northern Ireland."[270] Yet in adopting this perspective on the GFA, we encounter a problem, for this meant that, as Colin Harvey argues, "the contest of Northern Ireland has not ended."[271] The rhetoric and proposed institutions in the power-sharing agreement enshrine an approach to conflict resolution that involves the conversion of sites of contestation to sites of coexistence and/or collaboration, in a normative effort to build a lasting peace between communities in the country. Even in a site of contestation like the Northern Ireland Assembly, complicated mechanisms—from the d'Hondt system to PR STV voting— are designed to temper the zero-sum game of politics. Thus, one can conclude that the overall cohesion strategy of the Belfast Agreement was differentiation, underpinned by the institutionalizing of sites of coexistence and collaboration.

Elaborating on the causal hypotheses I pose in Figure 14, the Northern Irish case study analysis should find that ethnic tensions, on balance, have decreased. Accordingly, there should be limited success for the power-sharing regime in the long run. Because of the overall SSIs of coexistence and collaboration, the Good Friday Agreement, if implemented fully, would provide the conditions for a decrease in ethnic tensions. If the overall cohesion strategy of differentiation is implemented, case-specific factors will help determine whether or not there was an increase or decrease of intergroup animosities in Northern Ireland.

---

[269] See James Dingley, "Constructive Ambiguity and the Peace Process in Northern Ireland," *Low Intensity Conflict & Law Enforcement* 13, no. 1 (January 1, 2005): 1–23, https://doi.org/10.1080/09662840500223531 for the usage of the term "constructive ambiguity," and in his opinion, its negative impact on the Northern Irish peace process.

[270] Arthur Aughey, *The Politics of Northern Ireland: Beyond the Belfast Agreement* (London; New York: Routledge, 2005), 113.

[271] Colin Harvey quote from Aughey, 113.

4.5: *'Fighting For Peace' after Power-Sharing*

Simultaneous referenda on the Good Friday Agreement were held in northern and southern Ireland on May 22, 1998. Unionist reactions were mixed. Though David Trimble, leader of the UUP, claimed he secured the end of the Republic's territorial claims and recognition of "the territorial integrity of the United Kingdom," others like the Rev. Ian Paisley and his Democratic Unionist Party were unconvinced.[272] The DUP called the deal "treacherous" and was "nothing short of deception."[273] Paul Dixon notes how politicians like Tony Blair engaged in 'honorable deception' under the veil of the Agreement's ambiguity, to convince certain Conservatives and unionists, who "had supported the 'Yes' campaign in the referendum under the impression that decommissioning would take place."[274]

The republican movement, for their part, trusted in the Sinn Féin leadership, who reasoned that the Agreement was "weakening the British link while defending the rights of Irish men and women..."[275] Though splinter groups would contest the GFA, the Catholic community—both nationalist and republican—voted in a cohesive manner. For a moment, SF and the main Catholic nationalist party—the Social Democratic and Labour Party (SDLP)—worked in concert. The campaign was successful in both countries. With a record turnout in Northern Ireland of 81 percent, 71.1 percent voted in favor of the Agreement, and in the Republic, it was an overwhelming 94.4 percent.[276] However, as Aughey observes, "the overwhelming majority of nationalists voted yes but only a small majority of unionists did likewise."[277] This could be viewed as a harbinger of the unionist community's distrust of the GFA, but at the moment, the

---

[272] Hennessey, *The Northern Ireland Peace Process*, 190.

[273] Ibid.

[274] Paul Dixon, "Tony Blair's Honorable Deception: In Defense of the 'Dirty' Politics of the Northern Ireland Peace Process," in Charles I. Armstrong, David Herbert and Jan Erik Mustad, eds., *The Legacy of the Good Friday Agreement: Northern Irish Politics, Culture and Art after 1998*, Palgrave Studies in Compromise after Conflict (Cham, Switzerland: Palgrave Macmillan, 2019), 48.

[275] Hennessey, *The Northern Ireland Peace Process*, 189.

[276] Aughey, 96.

[277] Ibid.

referendum was considered a tremendous success in legitimizing the treaty and paving the way for peace.

Stumbling blocks came, and many hurdles had to be jumped. Elections for the first Assembly yielded electoral success for the two main pro-Agreement parties; the UUP and the SDLP. In a close third was the anti-Agreement DUP, and the republican pro-Agreement Sinn Féin in fourth. As Hennessy observes, it was the first time in Northern Irish history that a nationalist party received the most first preference votes, while also revealing a split in unionism.[278] The repeal of the Government of Ireland Act 1920 with the passing of the Northern Ireland Constitution Act 1998 enshrined the country's place in the Union, dependent on the consent of the people.[279] However, the new Stormont government could not sit, over disagreements between the UUP and Sinn Féin over the IRA's decommissioning. This coincided with an upsurge in ethnic tensions, including the Omagh bombing in August 1998, which killed 29 people.[280] This incident was the deadliest attack in the conflict's history. Multiple proposals, including the Hillsborough Declaration and Way Forward document, sought to outline a clear timeline on both paramilitary decommissioning and British troop withdrawals, but mutual distrust proved to be a stubborn barrier for mutual agreement.[281]

The St Andrews Agreement in 2006 ushered in a 'fresh start' to the peace process. In 2003, Northern Irish elections resulted in the anti-agreement DUP and the republican Sinn Féin gaining the first and second most votes, respectively. This posed a considerable clash that ultimately led to the collapse of power-sharing and direct rule from Westminster. The DUP refused to enter an agreement with SF because they viewed that the IRA was still too closely linked with the political party.[282] Sinn Féin, on the other hand, did not acknowledge the reformed police service—and refused to share power with the DUP, who did not acknowledge all aspects of the

---

[278] Hennessey, *The Northern Ireland Peace Process*, 195.

[279] Ibid., 196.

[280] "Omagh Bombing: Key Events before and after the Attack," *The Irish Times*, accessed March 5, 2021, https://www.irishtimes.com/news/ireland/irish-news/omagh-bombing-key-events-before-and-after-the-attack-1.3593660.

[281] Hennessey, *The Northern Ireland Peace Process*, 200-2.

[282] "What Is the St Andrews Agreement?," *The Guardian*, October 17, 2006, http://www.theguardian.com/politics/2006/oct/17/northernireland.devolution1.

Good Friday Agreement. Progress was made when the IRA completed its decommissioning process in 2005.[283] By the next year, a compromise agreement was struck, so that Sinn Féin would accept the Police Service of Northern Ireland (PSNI) and the DUP would accept all power-sharing institutions.[284] On May 8, 2007, a remarkable power-sharing government, with Ian Paisley as First Minister and Martin McGuinness as Deputy First Minister, was established.

Figure 15. Implementation of GFA 10 Years After Adoption[285]

Good Friday Agreement (1998-2007)	Implementation
Power-sharing Transitional Government	Full Implementation
Electoral/Political Party Reform	Full Implementation
Decentralization/Federalism	Full Implementation
Dispute Resolution Committee	Full Implementation
Judiciary Reform	Minimum Implementation
Paramilitary Groups	Intermediate Implementation
Education Reform	Full Implementation

[283] Christopher Riches and Jan Palmowski, "St Andrews Agreement," in *A Dictionary of Contemporary World History* (Oxford University Press, 2019), https://www.oxfordreference.com/view/10.1093/acref/9780191870903.001.0001/acref-9780191870903-e-2676.
[284] Ibid.
[285] Data from Joshi et al., "Annualized implementation."

Economic and Social Development	Full Implementation
Detailed Implementation Timeline	Full Implementation
GFA overall implementation score (out of 100)	**95.24**

The *Peace Accords Matrix* data for the Good Friday Agreement paints a much better picture for this power-sharing arrangement's implementation 10 years after its adoption than the Taif Accords. The coding shows that most parts of the agreement were implemented except "judiciary reform" and "paramilitary groups," which received a "minimum" and "intermediate" coding, respectively. To recall, the categories listed above are a selection of a broader list that this dataset codes for. Further, the GFA scores high marks in its overall implementation score, a sign that it has almost been fully implemented. This data corroborates the historical analysis of post-agreement Northern Ireland. Although there were many stumbling blocks for peace, both communities remained committed to the peace process. Even when power-sharing collapsed, steps were taken in the interim—like the decommissioning of the IRA—to induce cooperation between unlikely bedfellows: Martin McGuinness and Ian Paisley. To delve into the GFA implementation process, I take a look into anti-discrimination and employment policies in Northern Ireland, which under "Economic and Social Development," was coded as fully implemented.

4.6: *Anti-Discrimination and Economic Opportunities after Peace*

The "Rights, Safeguards and Equality of Opportunity" section of the GFA addresses economic issues in Northern Ireland, envisioning an aggressive government push for economic equality and development. In this respect, post-GFA economic policies sought to create sites of coexistence and collaboration in the pursuit of a differentiation cohesion strategy. Section 1 sets conditions for economic reform. Although it places the onus on the UK Government, the implementation of economic policies was "pending the devolution of powers to a new Northern Ireland Assembly."[286] This underpins the emphasis on sustaining the political power-sharing settlement to usher in economic stability and progress. The GFA further outlined a comprehensive "regional development strategy," with the goal of "tackling the problems of a divided society and social cohesion in urban, rural and border areas" through transport, physical infrastructure, resource development, and urban renewal.[287] This overall strategy would be intertwined with "short and medium term economic planning."[288] The economy was seen as a vehicle to promote a site of collaboration, in which the UK Government could claim they aimed to 'lift all boats' in Northern Ireland—Protestant and Catholic. This is an apparent assimilation strategy for the region's workforce.

As for economic equality, Section 2, subsection iii tackles "employment equality," a serious issue for nationalists:

> "(iii) measures on employment equality included in the recent White Paper ("Partnership for Equality") and covering the extension and strengthening of anti-discrimination legislation, a review of the national security aspects of the present fair employment legislation at the earliest possible time, a new more focused Targeting Social Need initiative and a range of measures aimed at combating unemployment and progressively eliminating the differential in unemployment rates between the two communities by targeting objective need."[289]

This section admits the historical economic gap between Catholics and Protestants in Northern Ireland. As a prevailing factor in NICRA and the Northern Ireland civil rights movement's rise in the late 1960s, unfair housing and employment practices added to Catholic grievances

---

[286] "The Belfast Agreement," *GOV.UK*, accessed March 4, 2021, https://www.gov.uk/government/publications/the-belfast-agreement, 23.

[287] Ibid.

[288] Ibid., 23.

[289] Ibid., 23-4.

over political representation.[290] For many, this economic disparity was the original issue of the Troubles, which was then obfuscated by an armed struggle and militant republicanism that sought Irish unification.

The Partnership for Equality White Paper, written in March 1998, projected the economic possibilities for Northern Ireland after peace. It takes the neoliberal, 'new' Labour view on work, stating that "the Government believes that everyone should have an opportunity to play a productive role in the economy. Unemployment is a major contributor to poverty and the result of unemployment is usually welfare dependency."[291] The paper proposes the implementation of two initiatives: the Policy Appraisal and Fair Treatment (PAFT) guidance, which "aims to ensure that equality considerations are taken into account in the mainstream of Government policies" and "Targeting Social Need (TSN)...directed at socio-economic disadvantage."[292] In assessing PAFT's successes and failures since its first iteration in 1994, the Government concluded that a "statutory obligation on public bodies" is needed to implement "equality of opportunity" guidelines.[293] This body, a "unified Equality Commission," would consolidate the Fair Employment Commission, Equal Opportunities Commission for Northern Ireland, Commission for Racial Equality for Northern Ireland, and the Northern Ireland Disability Council, and may deliberate on "the application of the concept of parity of esteem" in the law.[294] In addition, the Government proposes a "New TSN" with "specific initiatives to promote the 'social economy' by developing economic activity and indigenous job creation at the community level."[295] These efforts, such as "job subsidies," targeted investment in "identified disadvantaged areas," and "targeting of education resources," would be coordinated

---

[290] See "Northern Ireland: The Civil Rights Movement - CCEA - GCSE History Revision - CCEA," *BBC Bitesize,* accessed March 5, 2021, https://www.bbc.co.uk/bitesize/guides/z3w2mp3/revision/2; "About Us – Northern Ireland Civil Rights," accessed March 5, 2021, http://www.nicivilrights.org/about-us/.

[291] "CCRU: Equality; Employment - Partnership for Equality," accessed March 5, 2021, https://cain.ulster.ac.uk/ccru/equality/docs/pfe98.htm#views.

[292] Ibid., Chapter 4.1

[293] Ibid. 4.9-4.11

[294] Ibid., 4.12-14.

[295] Ibid., 4.17-19

in conjunction with the Department of Economic Development and Northern Ireland Office.[296]

Another facet of the Northern Irish economy this White Paper examines are the problems of "social exclusion"—or marginalized communities, in today's parlance. A new initiative for Northern Ireland, Promoting Social Inclusion (PSI) is proposed, to prevent social exclusion.[297] This initiative, as laid out in the paper, seems amorphous, as it seeks a "holistic approach, transcending bureaucratic demarcation lines" and will improve "mechanisms for integrating policies and programmes...and drawing up key indicators of social exclusion against which to monitor progress."[298] Throughout this document, a running theme is revealed. It is evident that the Blair Government sought an active role in re-shaping the Northern Irish economy. Once a site of contestation between ethnic-religious communities, Blair wished to transform it into a site of collaboration where *all* disadvantaged, regardless of region, are uplifted. If poverty purportedly causes terror in the minds of many British politicians, then economic uplift will take the wind out of IRA recruitment.

On balance, the aggressive equality and anti-discrimination effort in the workforce has been somewhat successful. R.D. Osborne comments on the effects of these policies five years after the GFA: "the operationalization of fair participation, through affirmative action agreements, helped directly in the process of producing greater equality in the employment profiles of Protestants and Catholics."[299] The Northern Ireland Executive's *Labour Force Survey Religion Report* conducted in 2017 marks considerable strides in employment percentage parity between Protestants and Catholics. Their data showed that the working-age economic activity rate for Protestants changed "from 76% in 1992 to 73% in 2017" while Catholics changed "from 66% in 1992 to 70% in 2017."[300] The unemployment rate for ages 16+ also reflected the closing gap between communities: Protestants

---

[296] Ibid.

[297] Ibid., 4.27-29.

[298] Ibid., 4.29.

[299] R. D. Osborne, "'Evidence' and Equality in Northern Ireland," *Evidence & Policy* 3, no. 1 (January 2007): 79–97, http://dx.doi.org/10.1332/174426407779702120, 90.

[300] "Labour Force Survey Religion Report 2017," *The Executive Office*, January 30, 2019, https://www.executiveoffice-ni.gov.uk/news/labour-force-survey-religion-report-2017., 5.

percentages changed "from 9% in 1992 to 4% in 2017" and for Catholics "from 18% in 1992 to 4% in 2017."[301] These numbers show that a trend of parity is emerging in employment in Northern Ireland. For the Northern Irish Executive, these statistics and metrics prove that the country is steadily addressing the GFA's concern for the employment disparities that were a factor in the Troubles.

Nevertheless, many commentators caution against using these figures to trumpet the complete success of the Northern Irish peace process. Commenting on these numbers, John Coakley warns that "it would be dangerous to jump to any political conclusions on the basis of these demographic developments," in questions about the future of Northern Ireland's constitutional status.[302] Economist Esmond Birnie is more optimistic, saying that "the jobs gap between the communities had now 'closed completely'."[303] But he too is cautious against a rosy view of Northern Ireland's situation, adding that "the disappearance of the unemployment difference by itself does not definitively prove that religious discrimination existed in the past has now been eliminated."[304] Certainly, this data, at face value, does not unequivocally demonstrate that religious discrimination in the workforce is no longer an issue—although certain groups may claim that in order to discontinue these policies. They do point to promising trends that a level of parity in employment is being reached in the late 2010s. Catholics are gaining more job opportunities and closing the gap. In my framework, I categorize this case as a mostly successful instance of implementing an envisioned site of collaboration and assimilation strategy in the GFA.

---

[301] Ibid.

[302] Suzanne McGonagle, "Almost Equal Numbers of Catholics and Protestants in Northern Ireland of Working Age for the First Time," *The Irish News*, February 1, 2019, http://www.irishnews.com/news/northernirelandnews/2019/02/01/news/almost-equal-numbers-of-catholics-and-protestants-in-northern-ireland-of-working-age-for-the-first-time-1541284/.

[303] "Protestant and Catholic Employment Rates Level for First Time in Northern Ireland," *Belfast Telegraph*, accessed March 11, 2021, https://www.belfasttelegraph.co.uk/news/northern-ireland/protestant-and-catholic-employment-rates-level-for-first-time-in-northern-ireland-35398733.html.

[304] Ibid.

4.7: *Decommissioning: Having a Bone to Pick With Everyone*

The decommissioning of paramilitary groups in Northern Ireland was a controversial issue for both communities, hindering aspects of the peace process. The GFA outlines protocols for decommissioning, which calls for the Independent International Commission on Decommissioning (IICD) to "[develop] schemes which can represent a workable basis for achieving the decommissioning of illegally-held arms in the possession of paramilitary groups."[305] An aggressive timeline is laid out, with the goal of "[achieving] the decommissioning of all paramilitary arms within two years following endorsement in referendums North and South of the agreement and in the context of the implementation of the overall settlement" and the enactment of a decommissioning scheme by the end of June 1998.[306] During the referendum campaign, decommissioning remained a sticking point for many unionists, who felt hesitant to vote for the power-sharing agreement if the IRA was still mobilized. As mentioned earlier, Blair used constructive ambiguity to placate unionist concerns—through half-lies. Though the GFA did pass, the issue of decommissioning derailed the beginnings of the new Stormont government.[307] Hence, it is evident that this became a site of contestation, even before the power-sharing arrangement's ratification.

Northern Ireland's Secretary of State promulgated the Decommissioning Scheme by the end of June, in accordance with the power-sharing agreement. The document specifies the process of decommissioning, to be overseen by the IICD.[308] Spearheaded by General John de Chastelain of Canada, this institutional arrangement involved members from Finland and the United

---

[305] "Northern Ireland Peace Agreement," 22.

[306] Ibid.

[307] See "Background" in "CAIN: Events: Peace: Brief Note on Decommissioning," accessed March 24, 2021, https://cain.ulster.ac.uk/events/peace/decommission.htm. This resource provides a brief background of the issue of decommissioning in the context of the Good Friday Agreement, including the failure to form the devolved government between 1998 to 2001, because of the UUP's objections to the IRA's intransigence on their process for dumping arms. This eventually led to First Minister David Trimble's resignation.

[308] Decommissioning Scheme in "CAIN: Events: Peace: Brief Note on Decommissioning," accessed March 24, 2021, https://cain.ulster.ac.uk/events/peace/decommission/nio290698.pdf.

States. This bolstered trust in the fair oversight of decommissioning for armed republican groups. The proposal further outlines policies of non-disclosure and confidentiality for the members of paramilitary groups partaking in arms dumps.[309] The Commission would facilitate this process, recording the specifications of the arms, and destroying them.[310] Progress for the enactment of these proposals, however, was not made after the ratification of the GFA. Unionists would have none of it and hindered the formation of a power-sharing government.

As a result, unionist and nationalist elements drew lines in the sand. As David Mitchell writes, the "Unionists' determination to pursue decommissioning stemmed from their perception of the immense ideological implications of weapons—silent or otherwise—remaining in the hands of their republican adversaries."[311] For the republican movement, "Sinn Féin adopted a two-pronged approach of, on the one hand, constructing a discourse of non-violent progress and momentum towards achieving republicanism's traditional goals, and on the other, keeping in faith with its militant tradition by (among other things) stalling on decommissioning."[312] This fortified their non-violence claims as they engaged in Northern Irish politics, yet maintained their militarism to placate loyal republican supporters. The UUP made its move, as its ministers in the Stormont Executive resigned *en masse* on October 18, 2001—throwing Northern Ireland's government in disarray.[313] This moment was a critical juncture for the power-sharing agreement's viability, as it threatened to derail it completely. Nevertheless, on October 23, 2001, the IRA, framing itself as the savior of the GFA, announced: "We have implemented the scheme agreed with the IICD in August. Our motivation is clear. This unprecedented move is to save the peace process and to persuade others

---

[309] Ibid., 3-6.

[310] Ibid., 5-6.

[311] David Mitchell, "Sticking to Their Guns? The Politics of Arms Decommissioning in Northern Ireland, 1998–2007," *Contemporary British History* 24, no. 3 (September 1, 2010): 341–61, https://doi.org/10.1080/13619462.2010.497253, 345.

[312] Ibid., 348.

[313] "CAIN: Chronology of the Conflict 2001," accessed March 25, 2021, https://cain.ulster.ac.uk/othelem/chron/ch01.htm#181001.

of our genuine intentions."[314] Up to this point, the IRA did not budge in its intransigence—but its leadership chose to begin decommissioning to further its 'two-pronged' approach when the unionists were on the verge of ripping up Northern Ireland's power-sharing institutions.

The precarious nature of peace was on full display in this power-sharing crisis. However, the IRA did begin the decommissioning process and continued the destruction of arms in 2002 and 2003. It is no coincidence that the IRA's decommissioning continued relatively smoothly as the 2003 Northern Ireland Assembly elections yielded favorable results for Sinn Féin, placing it as the leader of the Catholic bloc in Stormont for the first time in its electoral history.[315] Two years later (2005), the IRA officially ended its armed struggle:

> "The leadership of Oglaigh na hEireann has formally ordered an end to the armed campaign.
> This will take effect from 4pm [1600 BST] this afternoon [Thursday 28 July 2005].
> All IRA units have been ordered to dump arms.
> All Volunteers have been instructed to assist the development of purely political and democratic programmes through exclusively peaceful means.
> Volunteers must not engage in any other activities whatsoever."[316]

By September, the Commission notified the UK and Irish Governments that they verified the completion of the IRA's decommissioning: "We have determined that the IRA has met its commitment to put all arms beyond

---

[314] "CAIN: Events: Peace: Irish Republican Army (IRA) Statement, 23 October 2001," accessed March 25, 2021, https://cain.ulster.ac.uk/events/peace/docs/ira231001.htm.

[315] "Northern Ireland Assembly Elections 2003," accessed March 15, 2021, https://www.ark.ac.uk/elections/fa03.htm.

[316] "CAIN: Events: Peace: Irish Republican Army (IRA) Statement on the Ending of the Armed Campaign, (28 July 2005)," accessed March 25, 2021, https://cain.ulster.ac.uk/othelem/organ/ira/ira280705.htm.

use in a manner called for by the legislation."[317] Seven years after the power-sharing arrangement, the contentious issue of the IRA's demilitarization was laid to rest. Although smaller loyalist and fringe republican militias continued to decommission their arms between 2005 to 2010, the IICD officially ended its mandate in February 2010.

The Good Friday Agreement attempted to foster a site of collaboration, under the auspice of an international, independent body, to decommission paramilitary groups. It was soon clear that this area was a site of contestation for the main political actors in Northern Ireland. Mitchell describes this environment aptly: "In this context of threat, vulnerability and uncertainty, the decommissioning issue perpetuated the zero-sum thinking and communal mobilisation associated with earlier periods, with the political effect of polarisation."[318] This was the only way to properly assimilate violent actors into Northern Irish society. Eventually, progress was made as decommissioning proceeded with the IRA—trickling down to smaller loyalist groups, who felt pressure to disarm because their main enemy was no longer weaponized. Therefore, it is apparent that although a site of contestation arose when it was conceived as a site of collaboration, decommissioning was implemented in a limited fashion. What resulted was the 'state-in-your-lane' atmosphere of an SSI of coexistence. This shows the potential for one type of SSI to transition to another during the power-sharing implementation process. Likewise, the assimilation strategy, though polarizing during the process, ultimately succeeded in its aim to end the armed struggle and bring all those involved into a peaceful mode of operation.

4.8: *Ethnic Tensions?: What Polling Does (and Does Not) Suggest*

Public opinion polling in Northern Ireland is widespread and common because the country's political stakeholders have incentives to gauge the people's views on Irish unification. So numerous are the polls and their

---

[317] Independent International Commission on Decommissioning (IICD) statement, September 26, 2005, https://cain.ulster.ac.uk/events/peace/decommission/iicd260905.pdf.

[318] Mitchell, 356.

results that Gerry Moriarty, in his piece in the *Irish Times* quips, "you can almost pick your poll to support your point of view."[319] Some polls can seem like a tale of two cities. In February 2020 alone, a Lucid Talk poll found that "46.8% in Northern Ireland would vote to remain in the UK, while 45.4% would vote for a united Ireland," while Liverpool University and Britain's Economic and Social Research Council found that "just 29% of voters" would support Irish unity, and "52% against."[320] How could we, then, accurately gauge ethnic sentiments in Northern Ireland? Can we use polling data to show the extent to which there are ethnic tensions after the GFA? Yes, it is possible—but only with a healthy dose of skepticism and if interviews, incidents, and other reporting can supplement polling data.

Since the Good Friday Agreement, people's perceptions of identity have shifted as a unique 'North Irishness' has gained traction among both Protestant and Catholic communities. Jonathan Tonge and Raul Gomez conduct a statistical analysis on the Northern Ireland Life and Times annual survey to investigate sectarian identities, as it provides consistent polling data on questions of political affiliation, identity, and the constitution every year after the power-sharing agreement was struck, except 2011 (due to funding issues).[321] Their 2015 findings reveal that an emergent Northern Irish identity is developing in the country, despite the prevalence of the British-Irish ethnic and national dynamic in political rhetoric. Accordingly, they show that:

---

[319] Moriarty, "Shared Island."

[320] "Poll Shows Northern Ireland Majority against United Ireland," *Reuters*, February 18, 2020, https://www.reuters.com/article/us-britain-nireland-poll-idUSKBN20C0WI; "Northern Ireland Poll Shows 45.4% Back Irish Unity and 46.8% Support Union with UK," *Belfast Telegraph*, accessed February 25, 2021, https://www.belfasttelegraph.co.uk/news/northern-ireland/northern-ireland-poll-shows-454-back-irish-unity-and-468-support-union-with-uk-38989093.html.

[321] Jonathan Tonge and Raul Gomez, "Shared Identity and the End of Conflict? How Far Has a Common Sense of 'Northern Irishness' Replaced British or Irish Allegiances since the 1998 Good Friday Agreement?," *Irish Political Studies* 30, no. 2 (April 3, 2015): 276–98, https://doi.org/10.1080/07907184.2015.1023716; "NI Life and Times Survey - Political Attitudes," accessed February 24, 2021, https://www.ark.ac.uk/nilt/results/polatt.html#identity.

"British identity has declined since 2000 even though 2012 represents an increase on the immediately preceding years. Conversely, both Irish and Northern Irish identity have increased since 2000…If we look at the evolution of Northern Irishness for the two main communities, it is evident that most Protestants started declaring themselves Northern Irish after the first half of the 2000s while the opposite trend is observed among Catholics." [322]

One's sense of identity and the strength of their feelings of belonging is a precursor to ethnic tensions. If the prevailing ethnic identities are steadily muted by some shared 'Northern Irish' identity, it is reasonable to think that ethnic antagonisms in Northern Ireland are, on balance, in decline since the GFA power-sharing agreement.

Figure 16. Northern Ireland Political Attitudes, 2013-2019[323]

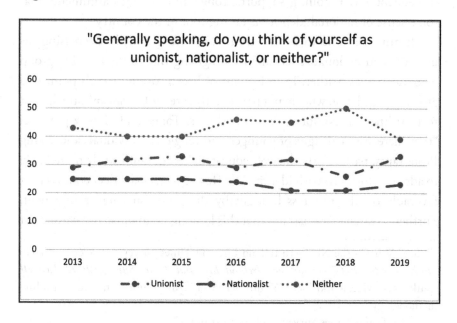

---

[322] Tonge and Gomez, 283.
[323] Data from "NI Life and Times Survey - Political Attitudes."

In general, these trends can be corroborated in more recent polling, since 2012. Created after the power-sharing agreement, the Northern Ireland Life and Times Survey conducts annual face-to-face interviews of 1800 respondents that reflect Northern Irish society.[324] Respondents were asked, "Generally speaking, do you think of yourself as a unionist, a nationalist, or neither?"[325] As shown in Figure 16, from 2013 to 2019, the "neither" response saw an overall slight increase in percentage. Conversely, both "unionist" and "nationalist" responses ever so slightly decreased. 2019 bucks the trend, as there was a marked decrease in respondents answering "neither" and a slight increase in both "unionist" and "nationalist" responses. This was caused by Brexit's centrality in the 2019 general election, which may have reawakened ethnic sentiments. However, as Kathy Hayward argues, the election results showed "there is a move to a centre ground" and "the overriding common feature of the centre ground is pro-remain."[326] Nevertheless, if one corresponds Unionism with Britishness, Nationalism with Irishness, and "neither" as a sense of Northern Irishness, then subsequent NILT polling supports Tonge and Gomez's arguments that some sense of national identity is taking root in the country.

Ethnic tensions in Northern Ireland are gradually decreasing, as unionist and nationalist sentiments are giving way to the growing group who identify as neither. Even in light of Brexit, overall trends point to a growing population who do not particularly care for Unionism's attachment to Britishness or Nationalism's to Irishness. Tonge and Gomez pinpoint "that there are clear signs of younger non-religious individuals and young Protestants, particularly the well-educated, being significantly more likely to adopt a Northern Irish identity."[327] This generational effect could reflect favorably on the progress brought by the power-sharing arrangement. Further research demonstrates that this leveling of unionist and nationalist

---

[324] See "What is the Northern Ireland Life and Times Survey?", *UK Data Archive Study Number 4767 – Northern Ireland Life and Times Survey, 2002*, https://sp.ukdataservice.ac.uk/doc/4767/mrdoc/pdf/4767userguide.pdf, for polling methodology.

[325] "NI Life and Times Survey - Political Attitudes."

[326] Katy Hayward, "The 2019 General Election in Northern Ireland: The Rise of the Centre Ground?," *The Political Quarterly* 91, no. 1 (2020): 49–55, https://doi.org/10.1111/1467-923X.12835, 54.

[327] Tonge and Gomez, 294.

ethnic identities and the emergence of a third, Northern Irish identity, can be attributed in large part to the GFA.

4.9: *Findings and Conclusions*

Figure 17. Northern Ireland Case Study Findings

Section of GFA	SSI		Cohesion Strategies		Observed Ethnic Tension
	Predicted	*Observed*	*Predicted*	*Observed*	
Anti-Discrimination/ Employment	Coexistence and Collaboration	Collaboration	Assimilation and Differentiation	Assimilation and Differentiation	Slight Decrease
De-commissioning	Collaboration	Contestation transition Coexistence	Assimilation	Assimilation	Slight Decrease

In the case of Northern Ireland, power-sharing was not embedded in the region's political legacy. The Northern Irish state preserved Protestant dominance in government, which among several factors, collapsed at the end of the 1960s—the beginnings of the Troubles. Various settlements throughout the violent conflict, though unsuccessful, built a foundation of trust between all political actors involved in Northern Ireland. This led to the creation and ratification of the Belfast Agreement in 1998. The recent history, post-agreement, attests to the hard-won peace being cultivated in the country. Many false starts and rock blocks ensnarled the Northern Irish peace process. But through the efforts of strong-willed politicians who were committed to peace, power-sharing institutions remain intact—unlike the Lebanese state.

Through this study, I confirm the relationship between SSIs and cohesion strategies, ethnic tensions, and the success or failure of power-sharing. Figure 17 provides a succinct overview of my case study. Through a textual analysis of the Good Friday Agreement, I categorize its sections into my typologies of SSIs and cohesion strategies, finding an overall SSI of coexistence and cohesion strategy of differentiation. Then, I engage in a process-tracing analysis of two particular sections: anti-discrimination and employment and decommissioning. Northern Ireland's anti-discrimination legislation and employment equality outcomes demonstrate success in implementing the envisioned sites of coexistence and collaboration, as well as the overall strategy of assimilation and differentiation. The case of decommissioning is of note since I conclude that although conceived as a site of collaboration, in reality, it became a site of contestation and then transitioned into a site of coexistence, after decommissioning ended. This demonstrates the fluid progression of SSIs as power-sharing regimes implement their policies. As for ethnic tensions, I found that there was a slight decrease in tensions since peace was achieved. Lastly, power-sharing has been implemented and the state, since its reconstitution, has been relatively stable—so I deem this a limited success. Overall, these findings confirm my hypotheses within the context of Northern Ireland.

CHAPTER 5

CONCLUSION: IS POWER-SHARING WORTH IT?

"But you see, it's not me, it's not my family / In your head, in your head they are fighting / With their tanks, and their bombs, and their bombs, and their guns / In your head, in your head they are crying"

— The Cranberries, *Zombie*, 1994[328]

"They said to you / Enough preaching, come dance with me a bit / Why are you frowning, come dance with me a bit / They taught you the anthem; they said your struggle is useful for the nation / They drugged you in the vein; they said your lethargy is useful for the nation."

— Mashrou' Leila, *Lil Watan*, 2013[329]

5.1: *Summary of Findings*

Figure 18. Summary of Case Study Findings

Case Study	Lebanon		Northern Ireland	
Within-Case Studies	Education	Economic Policy/ Displacement	Anti-Discrimination/ Employment	Decommissioning

---

[328] *The Cranberries – Zombie*, accessed March 9, 2021, https://genius.com/The-cranberries-zombie-lyrics.

[329] "Mashrou' Leila: Lil Watan (الأوطَن)," *Lebanese Arabic Institute* (blog), December 4, 2016, https://www.lebanesearabicinstitute.com/mashrou-leila-lil-watan/.

HI: SSI and Cohesion Strategies confirmed?	Yes	Yes	Yes	Yes (proved possibility of SSI *transition*)
H2: SSI-Cohesion Strategies and Ethnic Tensions confirmed?	Yes		Yes	
H3: Power-Sharing Outcome confirmed?	Yes		Yes	

This work endeavored to answer the question: To what extent do power-sharing arrangements affect ethnic tensions in post-conflict society? I conclude that power-sharing plays a definitive role in ethnic tensions and regime outcomes. To sum up, I reformulated Pierre Nora's *lieux de mémoire* to extrapolate a sites of social interactions (SSIs) model as a unit of analysis for post-conflict societies. Alongside a model of cohesion strategies that accounts for power-sharing institutional designs, I describe a causal logic by piecing together my proposed theoretical frameworks. They predict the increase or decrease of ethnic group animosities after power-sharing arrangements are instituted. According to my typology of SSIs, sites of contestation (zero-sum game) correspond to an increase in ethnic tensions. Conversely, sites of collaboration (shared space) correspond to a decrease in tensions. For sites of coexistence (tolerance/stay-in-your-own-lane), I hypothesize that ethnic antagonisms may increase or decrease, depending on case-specific conditions. As for cohesion strategies, I determine that assimilation—under a new national identity or a hegemonic ethnic identity—will increase tensions between ethnic rivals, while segregation—separation and bifurcation of nationality—yields a decrease in tensions. Differentiation, which pursues tolerance and pluralism, will either increase or decrease animosities, depending on specific factors. Lastly, I posit that SSIs and cohesion strategies that produce an increase in ethnic tensions through power-sharing will lead to the regime's long-term failure. On the other hand, SSIs and cohesion strategies that form a decrease will lead to a power-sharing regime's long-term success. Mixed ethnic animosities could yield limited failure or success depending on certain case factors.

Lebanon's history with power-sharing demonstrates that consociationalism had played a leading role in maintaining stability for that part of the world for centuries. Under the French mandate, these traditions of consociation were enshrined in the country's constitution, but presupposes a Maronite Catholic majority. During the 1960s and 70s, the government's political make-up became unsustainable demographically, which precipitated the Lebanese civil war. After years of turbulence, involving multiple intra- and interethnic conflicts and interventions from abroad, parties met at Taif, Saudi Arabia to strike a power-sharing agreement for a new Lebanon. In the power-sharing agreement, one can see an overall SSI of coexistence and cohesion strategies of assimilation and differentiation.

Next, I focused on two specific sections of Taif: namely, education and economic recovery/displacement. Many factors, after peace was achieved, led to weak implementation of the power-sharing agreement. Lebanese education, envisioned as a site of collaboration for an assimilation strategy, turned into a site of contestation, as religious leaders and partisan politics intervened in the building of curricula and textbooks. The effects are felt throughout the school system, showing disparities among sects and a lack of a truly national education program. As for the neoliberal economic reforms overseen by the new Lebanese government, corruption and clientelism tainted the coexistence and collaboration SSIs, creating a site of contestation. Displacement claims were filed through sectarian parties. War reconstruction, at least for Lebanese officials, meant raising the very sites of coexistence that Beirutis cherished before the war. My gauge of ethnic tensions found, in the same period after the reconstitution of Lebanon's government, that animosities have increased dramatically. Overall, it is evident that the Taif Accords failed to cultivate sites conducive to a decrease in ethnic tensions, resulting in Lebanon's power-sharing failure in the long run. My hypotheses are thus confirmed.

Northern Ireland, created in the aftermath of Irish independence, did not have a power-sharing tradition. Instead, it was configured to provide a majority ethnic-religious Protestant government. Conditions made the Protestant unionist hegemony over Stormont untenable in the 1960s, which led to the outbreak of the Troubles in 1972. As political violence and terrorism ebbed and flowed during this period, political actors from the UK, Ireland, and Northern Ireland proposed various power-sharing settlements—though all were unsuccessful. This changed in 1998, however, when the Belfast Agreement was struck on Good Friday. Composing of constitutional reconfigurations, international treaties, and the use of supranational bodies like the European Union, the GFA had immense breadth and depth.

In the power-sharing agreement, I found that it encoded overall SSIs of coexistence and contestation, as well as a cohesion strategy of differentiation. The concepts of 'parity of esteem' and 'mutual respect' guided policymakers' vision for Northern Ireland, as these ideas became institutionalized and manifested through these types of SSIs and the cohesion strategy. I examine two realms of the agreement: anti-discrimination legislation and economic equality, and decommissioning. The mostly successful implementation of sites of coexistence and collaboration in anti-discrimination and economic reform for Northern Ireland promised to decrease antagonisms. As for the issue of decommissioning, the GFA was idealistic in its proscription of a site of collaboration. It became a sticking point at the beginning of the Stormont government, causing power-sharing breaks in the first years of peace. However, by the time the IRA decommissioned fully, this sphere became a site of coexistence, which pursued an assimilation strategy for paramilitaries. For my analysis of sentiments, ethnic tensions in the country, on balance, decreased slightly. My hypotheses line up with the Northern Irish case study, further corroborating my conclusions in the Lebanese case.

My thesis proves a distinct causal chain between ethnic tensions and power-sharing success or failure, analyzed through the theoretical framework of sites of social interaction and cohesion strategies. Figure 18 neatly gathers my findings from each case study, comparing them to my hypotheses addressed in Chapter 2. On one hand, power-sharing arrangements with SSIs and cohesion strategies that promote an increase in ethnic tensions or fail to implement SSIs and cohesion strategies that would promote a decrease in animosities will falter in the long run. On the other hand, power-sharing including SSIs and cohesion strategies conducive to a decrease in ethnic tensions and that are successfully implemented will endure. In between these two conclusions, there are degrees of the increase or decrease of ethnic animosity in post-conflict society and degrees of success or failure (limited success or failure, as I describe) in power-sharing regimes. In the case of decommissioning, I conclude that there is a possibility for SSIs to *transition* during the implementation process of a power-sharing agreement, contingent upon certain factors. This variation of my hypothesis should be acknowledged but does not detract from its overall viability to explain this phenomenon. Hence, I demonstrate my three hypotheses' explanatory power in my comprehensive comparative study.

Power-sharing arrangements impact a divided society's ethnic relations through the mechanisms of sites of social interaction and cohesion strategies. The outcome of power-sharing, in a broad sense, is a function of the extent to which ethnic tensions are salient in a post-conflict society. The Lebanon and Northern Ireland cases illustrate similar paths, but drastic differences—due, in large part, to each country's power-sharing arrangements. Each arrangement proscribes a different societal make-up (SSIs) and institutional design (cohesion strategies), to achieve stability after a civil war. While the Taif Accords was minimally implemented, the GFA was mostly implemented. The missing key in understanding power-sharing and ethnic tensions lie in this theory of society, institutional design, and ethnic identity.

5.2: *Scholarly and Practical Implications*

I am careful not to make broad-stroke conclusions in the field of ethnic conflict. The SSI and cohesion strategies model should be treated as one of many lenses to analyze power-sharing and ethnic conflict after peace is achieved in divided societies. These frameworks can be a touchstone for new research or analyzing previous works. Michael Kerr, for instance, uses the same cases to investigate the role of external powers in each polity's relative failure and success. He argues: "As far as consociation in Northern Ireland

and Lebanon is concerned, exogenous pressures have been the determining factors when evaluating consociation's chances of long-term success," a reasonable conclusion after my own study of both countries.[330] On the surface, our conclusions may look incompatible. However, my framework may actually supplement Kerr's work, as future scholarship can analyze the extent to which external powers influence the creation or dissolution of certain SSIs and cohesion strategies conducive to ethnic tensions increase or decrease. One may find that an external power's influence may affect ethnic tensions and alter the trajectory of power-sharing arrangements. Simply put, this framework lends itself for use in a post-conflict setting, where it can assist scholars in their studies of divided societies. As more of these constitutional remedies are being instituted, there is a greater need to study the effects of these political institutions. Lebanon and Northern Ireland are cases that paralleled in ethnic-religious conflict, but drastically differ in outcomes.

I believe SSIs and cohesion strategies can aid scholars as they study other causal factors that contribute to power-sharing's success or failure. For example, an in-depth case analysis of Belgium's power-sharing regime can use the SSI and cohesion strategies framework to assess how the political institutions have shaped Belgian society.[331] A scholar may look into a particular causal variable in a multi-ethnic society—like Singapore's adoption of English as the state's *lingua franca*—to determine how it aided in the country's cohesion strategy.[332] Though my theoretical framework

---

[330] Michael Kerr, *Imposing Power-Sharing: Conflict and Coexistence in Northern Ireland and Lebanon* (Dublin, 2006), http://hdl.handle.net/2027/mdp.39015064694444, 40.

[331] See Marc Hooghe and Kris Deschouwer, "Veto Players and Electoral Reform in Belgium," *West European Politics* 34, no. 3 (May 1, 2011): 626–43, https://doi.org/1 0.1080/01402382.2011.555987. Their discussion about the electoral reform process could lend itself to an examination of why certain reforms have failed while others have succeeded through my conceptual schemas.

[332] See Chapter 1, "Language Policy in Singapore: English, Singlish, and the Mother Tongues" in Lionel Wee, *The Singlish Controversy: Language, Culture and Identity in a Globalizing World* (Cambridge: Cambridge University Press, 2018), https://doi.org/10.1017/9781316855331. On face value, I can hypothesize that Singapore's language policy pursues an assimilation cohesion strategy through a site of coexistence. Scholars can study specific aspects of an ethnically-diverse society, like language, through my theory.

was premised on the study of power-sharing and ethnic tensions, there is room for the typologies established in my thesis to be appropriated to ask broader questions about the relationship between institutions and society—ethnically divided or not.

This examination adds to the rich body of work analyzing the effects of power-sharing arrangements. I prove that power-sharing institutions carry weight in future ethnic tensions and possibly, future sources of ethnic conflict. Although power-sharing may achieve peace in the short run, it may pose governing challenges in the future if ethnic tensions remain high and if sites of contestation are dominant in a divided society. This aligns with Roeder and Rothchild's views on power-sharing: "The very same institutions that provide an attractive basis to end a conflict in an ethnically divided country are likely to hinder the consolidation of peace and democracy over the longer term."[333] In contrast, my theoretical frameworks conflict with other scholars' theoretical findings on consociationalism, such as Lijphart and Horowitz.[334] My focus is on societal impacts of institutions, rather than ideal institutional designs per se.

In particular, this study calls into question Lijphart's original theories of consociational democracy, especially in its favorable view of elite coalition-building. His notion of a grand coalition is premised on elite compromise "because it minimizes the risk of being deceived by the other parties or by one's own undue optimism concerning *their* willingness to be accommodating."[335] But if this space is viewed as a site of contestation, where a zero-sum game takes place, cooperation becomes only an ideal. How can a system premised on compromise be sustainable for a state's long-term viability, when by the nature of the political institutions, they are sites of contestation? Even after both Taif and the GFA implemented political mechanisms that, in theory, tempered this winner-loser dynamic, power-sharing was still fraught with ethnic tension in the political sphere.

---

[333] Donald Rothchild and Philip Roeder, "Dilemmas of State-Building in Divided Societies," in Roeder and Rothchild, *Sustainable Peace*, 6.

[334] See Arend Lijphart, "Consociational Democracy," in *The Oxford Companion to Comparative Politics* (Oxford University Press, 2012), https://www.oxfordreference.com/view/10.1093/acref/9780199738595.001.0001/acref-9780199738595-e-95; Donald L. Horowitz, *Ethnic Groups in Conflict* (Berkeley: University of California Press, 1985).

[335] Lijphart, *Democracy in Plural Societies*, 31.

Older theories of consociation can lend themselves to theoretical and empirical study in the SSIs and cohesion strategies framework—and may lead to institutional design improvements for divided societies.

In practice, policymakers must be cognizant of the long-term impact that power-sharing agreements have on a polity. In a sense, the designers of consociational constitutions have a role to play in influencing the formation or re-formation of ethnic identities in post-conflict societies. Policymakers should view power-sharing through a macro-oriented lens. They should try to account for how political institutions influence practices and behaviors that trickle down to the societal level. For example, the Lebanese power-sharing agreement guaranteed the right for religious notables to provide education, but in a different section, it calls for universal education under a unifying, national curriculum. If policymakers were aware of the repercussions of this underlying contradiction on education policy when they wrote it, they should not be shocked to see those religious leaders stymie education reform in the country. Surely, I have the valuable tool of hindsight, but if these texts are laid out with more intentionality—considering SSIs, cohesion strategies, and its effects of ethnic tensions—power-sharing can be a more viable tool for long-term stability in a divided society.

Although the full implementation of power-sharing settlements seems rare, agreements that consider society-wide action (Northern Ireland) will fare better than strictly political designs. Policymakers should anticipate roadblocks in power-sharing implementation. There is always wriggle room in these negotiations, either for good or ill, but if implementation is to be successful, politicians must be held accountable. Both Lebanon and Northern Ireland suffered from this problem. The lack of accountability was in full display in the aftermath of the 2020 Beirut port explosion, but many Lebanese people already knew that corruption and illegal enrichment go hand in hand in that country's politics.[336] After charges were brought against former prime minister Hassan Diab, his legal counsel "accused the judge of violating the Constitution by circumventing the Parliament with his latest actions and suggested that the judge did not have the authority

---

[336] See "Corruption Is Endemic in Lebanon's Political System," *Transparency. org*, accessed March 28, 2021, https://www.transparency.org/en/blog/corruption-is-endemic-in-lebanons-political-system-the-imf-can-help-change-that.

to charge a prime minister.[337] The Stormont government, to a lesser extent, has had issues with accountability in the Executive.[338] The 2012 Renewable Heat Incentive, headed by First Minister Arlene Foster, came under fire for mismanagement and allegations of corruption. Although an independent inquiry absolved the First Minister of corruption, the report found incompetence and mismanagement in Stormont: "an accumulation of errors and omissions over time and a failure of attention, on the part of all those involved in their differing roles, to identify the existence, significance or implications of those errors and omissions."[339]

As seen in Lebanon and Northern Ireland, power-sharing is never fully manifested in its theoretical forms or as proscribed by political scientists. Rather, it is a product of arduous negotiations and compromises, which may hinder the development of a social fabric for post-conflict societies in the long run. It is true especially if negotiations are elite-driven, top-down approaches, instead of a bottom-up, democratic consent-based agreement. This form of power-sharing gives citizens the power to hold politicians accountable for their actions, especially short-sighted political calculations that jeopardize peace. Stable power-sharing should lend itself to democratic norms. Though I may sound idealistic, I do not believe these two concepts are contradictory. In fact, I would argue that they are supplemental to post-conflict regime stability.

I am no philosopher or politician—but as an academic, I can conclude that power-sharing institutions have a clear and defined normative impact on society and identity. This is not an innovation of thought, of course. Nonetheless, SSIs and cohesion strategies provide key insights into this powerful relationship. Political actors should be cognizant, especially when crafting legislation and political institutions, of the long-term ramifications of their decisions. In this case, it is one thing to write down statistical

---

[337] Ben Hubbard, "Lebanon Prime Minister Charged With Negligence in Beirut Blast," *The New York Times*, December 10, 2020, https://www.nytimes.com/2020/12/10/world/middleeast/beirut-explosion-charges.html.

[338] See "Northern Ireland: Restoration of the Power-Sharing Executive," *The Institute for Government*, January 13, 2020, https://www.instituteforgovernment.org.uk/explainers/northern-ireland-restoration-power-sharing-executive.

[339] "Cash-for-Ash Inquiry Delivers Damning Indictment of Stormont Incompetence," *The Guardian*, March 13, 2020, http://www.theguardian.com/uk-news/2020/mar/13/cash-for-ash-inquiry-delivers-damning-indictment-of-stormont-incompetence.

electoral formulas and high-minded ideals like 'justice' and 'peace' on a piece of paper—it is another to actually enact peace-building institutions and strategies in a war-torn society. Sure, it is a tall order to ask leaders to achieve these things in a lifetime—but it is still something that the people must demand.

5.3: *Remaining Questions*

My research establishes a causal relationship between sites of social interaction and cohesion strategies in power-sharing arrangements and the increase or decrease in ethnic tensions in a divided society. There are plenty of questions to explore because of this investigation. Within both case studies, recent developments in Lebanon and Northern Ireland raise important questions about the future of power-sharing in those countries. How has the influx of Syrian refugees challenged the already fragile SSIs in Lebanon? What is the interplay between the shifting demographics in Lebanon and the cohesion strategies the government pursues? In Northern Ireland, how will Brexit affect the region's cohesion strategy of 'parity of esteem'? What is the role of Northern Irish civil society and grassroots organizations in cultivating sites of collaboration, integral to reducing ethnic tensions? Lebanon and Northern Ireland face dramatic critical junctures in 2021—and the decisions of political actors and the people may chart a new course for power-sharing in these countries.

There are also general, enduring questions in this field that my work raises. To what extent do international powers affect the outcomes of power-sharing agreements and their implementation? What role do modernization and secularism play in reinforcing ethnic-religious identities? How has the specter of colonialism haunted these violent conflicts and their power-sharing agreements? How are institutions—meant to function or operate in one way—altered, manipulated, or co-opted to advance political goals in ways that were not anticipated? What role does the population have in influencing power-sharing and coalition building? How can sites of social interaction and cohesion strategies transform ethnic identities in general? Can institutions remold ethnic, linguistic, religious, and racial identities? In this discussion, we cannot ignore the normative questions this study raises. Is power-sharing a preferred solution to ethnic conflict, if it may lead to an increase of ethnic tensions in the long run? Can power-sharing institutions that achieve peace be scrapped for other political arrangements that may be more democratic in the future?

5.4: *Final Remarks*

Let's return to where we left off, in our "tale of two taxi drivers": Abu George and David. In the first chapter, we asked if we "can view power-sharing through the rearview window?" The short answer is yes—and no. This work has studied power-sharing arrangements in Northern Ireland and Lebanon knowing that there has been a sizeable gap between each peace agreement's ratification and today's power-sharing outcomes. Yet, I don't think we can fully view power-sharing agreements as a thing of the past, especially in these two countries. In fact, for our two taxi drivers, the legacy of power-sharing is ever-present. For them, it's not about viewing their society behind the rearview mirror—it's about what's in front of them through the windshield. David sees Belfast's UDA murals, adorned with the Union Jack and the colorful images of loyalist defenders dressed in their opaque sunglasses and bright berets—indeed, the great embodiment of 'No Surrender' in the face of the 'greening' of Northern Ireland. Abu George sees Beirut's bombed-out Holiday Inn—once a testament to the 'Paris of the Middle East,' now dilapidated, riddled by the scars of sniper fire and shelling, towering high above a crippled city—as the Security Forces guard this edifice of Lebanon's circular possibilities: of what was and what is a condition of suffering. For all my theoretical squabbling, posing 'ifs' and forming hypotheses, the real 'research' question is quite simple, at least for our taxi drivers: was power-sharing worth it?

Power-sharing is an institutional concept that projects itself onto post-conflict societies, emanating practices and behaviors that influence the rise and fall of ethnic divisions. Ethnicity is not constant. Identity is malleable. Ethnic identity is thus contingent. Many scholars have explored these notions and proven, both theoretically and empirically, that these are the logics behind nation-ness. To some, this analysis of identity seems as though humans are wishy-washy, ever-changing, and inconstant. Yet, as it is made evident in this study, the contemporary world order is underpinned by the idea of nations and states. The bloodiest conflicts post-World War

II and into this present century involve these fundamental questions of national identity. What is championed by the cases of Northern Ireland and Lebanon, at least traditionally, is how these two countries ended their internal conflict: through power-sharing institutions.

In a post-Cold War era of resurgent liberal internationalism, the concept of power-sharing was lauded by many theoreticians and practitioners of international affairs as a means of promoting peaceful, stable democracy in war-torn divided societies. Such areas, like Lebanon and Northern Ireland, cannot even agree on basic things like a flag or symbol, or a national language or 'character,' yet they have found a path towards coexistence. With the guiding hand of other countries, rival groups who seemed like they want to maim and kill the 'other' in a primordial, tribe-like matter found themselves sitting at the negotiation table, signing a new era of peace for their grateful nations. Or so they believed.

Consociational democracy that is intentionally implemented, in practice, has not had too many successes. Even in the cases that may seem relatively successful, power-sharing encounters serious challenges not only in implementation but in its own preservation. Mechanisms designed to do so and so or modify behavior in such a manner get co-opted and instrumentalized for political expediency. This may be a pessimistic view of power-sharing, albeit grounded in this study's analysis of Lebanon and Northern Ireland.

But, as much as I can diminish these power-sharing agreements for not living up to the promise that they may have held, power-sharing *does* accomplish two laudable objectives: peace and democracy. The effects of 'negative' peace, or the absence of war, truly changed the fabric of the two countries we have examined. In Lebanon, negative peace charted a neoliberal path in its economic development and reconstruction, as the likes of Rafik Hariri tried to transform Beirut from a warzone into a center of luxury. But that allure is long forgotten. Northern Ireland, similarly, has experienced positive economic growth, as the city of Belfast has flourished in the tourist and service industries. But Brexit throws all of this up in the air, for the time being.

We cannot underestimate the normative impact of power-sharing institutions on society. Perhaps, as political scientists, we take that for granted. When institutions are held up to a magnifying glass, not just in its political consequences, but in its effects on everyday life, we get a glimpse of how something as 'essential' or 'inherent' as ethnic, religious, political, or linguistic identity can be molded by socio-political structures and behaviors. After all, institutions ultimately institutionalize *ideas*—in some cases, what *is*, in others, what *ought* to be. As humans who hold identities, as citizens who participate in politics, and as members of a cohesive, common unit known as society, we must challenge, scrutinize, repudiate, and justify the institutions that we create. Not just for the sake of the people of Northern Ireland and Lebanon, or of David and Abu George. For our own.

BIBLIOGRAPHY

"'158 Security-Related Deaths' since Good Friday Agreement." *BBC News*. Accessed February 22, 2021. https://www.bbc.com/news/uk-northern-ireland-43862294.

"2020 Census Questions: Hispanic Origin." *2020Census.gov*. Accessed November 10, 2020. https://2020census.gov/en/about-questions/hispanic-origin.html.

"A Breakthrough for Language Rights in Northern Ireland." *OHRH*, February 18, 2020. https://ohrh.law.ox.ac.uk/a-breakthrough-for-language-rights-in-northern-ireland/.

"About the Ulster Covenant." *nidirect*, December 1, 2015. https://www.nidirect.gov.uk/articles/about-ulster-covenant.

"About Us – Northern Ireland Civil Rights." Accessed March 5, 2021. http://www.nicivilrights.org/about-us/.

Acharya, Avidit, David D. Laitin, and Anna Zhang. "'Sons of the Soil': A Model of Assimilation and Population Control." *Journal of Theoretical Politics* 30, no. 2 (2018): 184–223. https://doi.org/10.1177/0951629817737858.

Akar, Bassel, and Mara Albrecht. "Influences of Nationalisms on Citizenship Education: Revealing a 'Dark Side' in Lebanon." *Nations and Nationalism* 23, no. 3 (2017): 547–70. https://doi.org/10.1111/nana.12316.

Anderson, Benedict R. *Imagined Communities: Reflections on the Origin and Spread of Nationalism*. Rev. ed. London; New York: Verso, 2006.

Andeweg, Rudy B. "Consociationalism." In *International Encyclopedia of the Social & Behavioral Sciences (Second Edition)*, edited by James D. Wright, 692–94. Oxford: Elsevier, 2015. https://doi.org/10.1016/B978-0-08-097086-8.93025-3.

Anter, Andreas. "The Modern State and Its Monopoly on Violence." The Oxford Handbook of Max Weber, March 5, 2020. https://doi.org/10.1093/oxfordhb/9780190679545.013.13.

Armstrong, Charles I., David Herbert, and Jan Erik Mustad, Editors. *The Legacy of the Good Friday Agreement: Northern Irish Politics, Culture and Art after 1998.* Palgrave Studies in Compromise after Conflict. Cham, Switzerland: Palgrave Macmillan, 2019.

Arsan, Andrew. *Lebanon: A Country in Fragments.* London: Hurst & Company, 2018.

Arthur, Paul. "Northern Ireland." In *A Concise Oxford Dictionary of Politics and International Relations.* Oxford University Press, 2018. https://www. oxfordreference.com/view/10.1093/acref/9780199670840.001.0001/ acref-9780199670840-e-916.

Assaf, Nayla. "Green Line Lives on in Minds of Beirut's Taxi Drivers," *The Daily Star Newspaper - Lebanon.* October 13, 2003. https://www. dailystar.com.lb//News/Lebanon-News/2003/Oct-13/40396-green-line-lives-on-in-minds-of-beiruts-taxi-drivers.ashx.

Aughey, Arthur. *The Politics of Northern Ireland: Beyond the Belfast Agreement.* London ; New York: Routledge, 2005.

Bakri, Nada, and Graham Bowley. "Confrontation in Lebanon Appears to Escalate." *The New York Times,* May 8, 2008. https://www.nytimes. com/2008/05/08/world/middleeast/09lebanon.html.

Bakri, Nada, and Alan Cowell. "Lebanese Reach Agreement to Resolve 18-Month Political Crisis." *The New York Times,* May 21, 2008. https://www.nytimes.com/2008/05/21/world/africa/21iht-lebanon.4.13105564.html.

Baquiano, Marshaley J. "Intergroup Positioning in Peace Negotiations: The Bangsamoro Peace Talks in the Philippines." *Peace and Conflict: Journal of Peace Psychology* 25, no. 3 (August 2019): 234–45. http:// dx.doi.org/10.1037/pac0000360.

Bardon, Jonathan. *A History of Ulster.* New updated ed. Belfast, Northern Ireland: Blackstaff Press, 2001.

Baytiyeh, Hoda. "Has the Educational System in Lebanon Contributed to the Growing Sectarian Divisions?" *Education and Urban Society* 49, no. 5 (June 1, 2017): 546–59. https://doi.org/10.1177/0013124516645163.

Bazzi, Mohamad. "The Corrupt Political Class That Broke Lebanon," *Foreign Affairs,* December 8, 2020. https://www.foreignaffairs.com/ articles/lebanon/2020-08-14/corrupt-political-class-broke-lebanon.

Bernstein, Richard J. "Cultural Pluralism." *Philosophy & Social Criticism* 41, no. 4–5 (May 1, 2015): 347–56. https://doi. org/10.1177/0191453714564855.

Bew, Paul. *Northern Ireland 1921-1994: Political Forces and Social Classes.* London: Serif, 1995.

Biggar, Hugh. "The Murals on Belfast's 'Peace Walls' Offer an Illustrated History of the Troubles." *Washington Post.* Accessed March 4, 2021. https://www.washingtonpost.com/lifestyle/travel/the-murals-on-belfasts-peace-walls-offer-an-illustrated-history-of-the-troubles/2018/08/15/4c993480-9cca-11e8-8d5e-c6c594024954_story.html.

Bogaards, Matthijs. "Consociationalism and Centripetalism: Friends or Foes?" *Swiss Political Science Review* 25, no. 4 (2019): 519–37. https://doi.org/10.1111/spsr.12371.

Bormann, Nils-Christian, Lars-Erik Cederman, Scott Gates, Benjamin A. T. Graham, Simon Hug, Kaare W. Strøm, and Julian Wucherpfennig. "Power Sharing: Institutions, Behavior, and Peace." *American Journal of Political Science* 63, no. 1 (2019): 84–100.

Bradley, Charlie. "Census 2021 Warning as Survey Could Lead to UK Split: 'Referendum Will Happen!'" *Express.co.uk*, March 20, 2021. https://www.express.co.uk/news/uk/1412629/census-2021-news-survey-uk-northern-ireland-referendum-brexit-deadline-spt.

Brewster, Jack. "Senate Reaches Power-Sharing Agreement And Democrats Take Over Committees." *Forbes.* Accessed March 25, 2021. https://www.forbes.com/sites/jackbrewster/2021/02/03/senate-reaches-power-sharing-agreement-and-democrats-take-over-committees/.

"Brexit Is Just Weeks Old, and It's Already Threatening Fragile Political Stability in Northern Ireland." *CNN.* Accessed February 22, 2021. https://www.cnn.com/2021/02/06/uk/brexit-northern-ireland-violence-threat-intl/index.html.

"Brexit: Loyalist Paramilitary Groups Renounce Good Friday Agreement," *The* Guardian, March 4, 2021. http://www.theguardian.com/uk-news/2021/mar/04/brexit-northern-ireland-loyalist-armies-renounce-good-friday-agreement.

"Bunreacht Na HÉireann (Constitution of Ireland)." Accessed March 1, 2021. https://celt.ucc.ie/published/E900003-005/text002.html.

Byman, Daniel. *Keeping the Peace: Lasting Solutions to Ethnic Conflicts.* Baltimore: Johns Hopkins University Press, 2002.

"CAIN: Chronology of the Conflict 2001." Accessed March 24, 2021. https://cain.ulster.ac.uk/othelem/chron/ch01.htm#181001.

"CAIN: Conflict in Northern Ireland: A Background Essay." Accessed February 24, 2021. https://cain.ulster.ac.uk/othelem/facets.htm#chap2.

"CAIN: Events: Peace: Brief Note on Decommissioning." Accessed March 24, 2021. https://cain.ulster.ac.uk/events/peace/decommission.htm.

"CAIN: Events: Peace: Irish Republican Army (IRA) Statement, 23 October 2001." Accessed March 24, 2021. https://cain.ulster.ac.uk/events/peace/docs/ira231001.htm.

"CAIN: Events: Peace: Irish Republican Army (IRA) Statement on the Ending of the Armed Campaign, (28 July 2005)." Accessed March 25, 2021. https://cain.ulster.ac.uk/othelem/organ/ira/ira280705.htm.

"CAIN: Events: The Sunningdale Agreement - Chronology of Main Events." Accessed February 24, 2021. https://cain.ulster.ac.uk/events/sunningdale/chron.htm.

Calame, Jon. *Divided Cities: Belfast, Beirut, Jerusalem, Mostar, and Nicosia*. City in the Twenty-First Century Book Series. Philadelphia: University of Pennsylvania Press, 2009.

Cammett, Melani, and Sukriti Issar. "Bricks and Mortar Clientelism: Sectarianism and the Logics of Welfare Allocation in Lebanon." *World Politics* 62, no. 3 (July 2010): 381–421. https://doi.org/10.1017/S0043887110000080.

"Cash-for-Ash Inquiry Delivers Damning Indictment of Stormont Incompetence," *The Guardian*, March 13, 2020. http://www.theguardian.com/uk-news/2020/mar/13/cash-for-ash-inquiry-delivers-damning-indictment-of-stormont-incompetence.

"CCRU: Equality; Employment - Partnership for Equality." Accessed March 5, 2021. https://cain.ulster.ac.uk/ccru/equality/docs/pfe98.htm#views.

Coakley, John. "National Identity in Northern Ireland: Stability or Change?" *Nations and Nationalism* 13, no. 4 (2007): 573–97. https://doi.org/10.1111/j.1469-8129.2007.00316.x.

Connor, Walker. "Nation-Building or Nation-Destroying?" *World Politics* 24, no. 3 (1972): 319–55. https://doi.org/10.2307/2009753.

———. "Terminological Chaos ('A Nation Is a Nation, Is a State, Is an Ethnic Group, Is a ...')." In *Ethnonationalism*, 89–117. The Quest for Understanding. Princeton University Press, 1994. https://doi.org/10.2307/j.ctv39x5s6.8.

Coogan, Tim Pat. *The Troubles: Ireland's Ordeal 1966-1996 and the Search for Peace*. Boulder, Colo.: Roberts Rinehart Publishers, 1997.

Cook, Steven A. "Lebanon as We Know It Is Dying." *Foreign Policy*. Accessed January 4, 2021. https://foreignpolicy.com/2020/07/30/lebanon-as-we-know-it-is-dying/.

Cordell, Karl. *Ethnic Conflict: Causes, Consequences, and Responses*. Cambridge; Malden, MA: Polity, 2009.

Cornish, Chloe. "Currency Crisis Leaves Lebanese Cupboards Bare," *Financial Times*, February 21, 2021. https://www.ft.com/content/69e1e040-d8d7-494e-9a90-6f02f68f0bf7.

"Corruption Is Endemic in Lebanon's Political System." *Transparency.org*. Accessed March 28, 2021. https://www.transparency.org/en/blog/corruption-is-endemic-in-lebanons-political-system-the-imf-can-help-change-that.

Cronin-Furman, Kate. "China Has Chosen Cultural Genocide in Xinjiang—For Now." *Foreign Policy*. Accessed January 10, 2021. https://foreignpolicy.com/2018/09/19/china-has-chosen-cultural-genocide-in-xinjiang-for-now/.

"'Dark Tourism' Booms at Northern Ireland's Troubles Museums." *BBC News*. Accessed March 4, 2021. https://www.bbc.com/news/uk-northern-ireland-46046674.

Dingley, James. "Constructive Ambiguity and the Peace Process in Northern Ireland." *Low Intensity Conflict & Law Enforcement* 13, no. 1 (January 1, 2005): 1–23. https://doi.org/10.1080/09662840500223531.

Dionne Jr., E. J. "BATTLES PICK UP ON BEIRUT'S GREEN LINE." *The New York Times*, February 27, 1984. https://www.nytimes.com/1984/02/27/world/battles-pick-up-on-beirut-s-green-line.html.

"Doha Agreement on the Results of the Lebanese National Dialogue Conference | UN Peacemaker." Accessed January 4, 2021. https://peacemaker.un.org/lebanon-dohaagreement2008.

Embong, Abdul Rahman. "The Culture and Practice of Pluralism in Postcolonial Malaysia." In *The Politics of Multiculturalism*, edited by Robert W. Hefner, 59–85. Pluralism and Citizenship in Malaysia,

Singapore, and Indonesia. University of Hawai'i Press, 2001. https://www.jstor.org/stable/j.ctt6wqpj7.5.

"External Evaluation - Indonesia." *Center for Civic Education*. Accessed January 8, 2021. https://www.civiced.org/civitas/program/research-and-evaluation/indonesia.

Fawaz, Mona, Mona Harb, and Ahmad Gharbieh. "Living Beirut's Security Zones: An Investigation of the Modalities and Practice of Urban Security: Living Beirut's Security Zones." *City & Society* 24, no. 2 (August 2012): 173–95. https://doi.org/10.1111/j.1548-744X.2012.01074.x.

Frayha, Nemer. "Education and Social Cohesion in Lebanon." *Prospects* 33, no. 1 (March 1, 2003): 77–88. https://doi.org/10.1023/A:1022664415479.

———. "Pressure Groups, Education Policy, and Curriculum Development in Lebanon: A Policymaker's Retrospective and Introspective Standpoint." *Education and the Arab "World": Political Projects, Struggles, and Geometries of Power*.

Friedman, Thomas L. *From Beirut to Jerusalem: Updated with a New Chapter*. New York: Anchor Books, Doubleday, 1995.

———. "U.S. Hails Lebanon Accord and Urges Support." *The New York Times*, October 24, 1989. https://www.nytimes.com/1989/10/24/world/us-hails-lebanon-accord-and-urges-support.html.

Geertz, Clifford. "What Is a Country If It Is Not a Nation?" *The Brown Journal of World Affairs* 4, no. 2 (1997): 235–47.

Gellner, Ernest. *Nations and Nationalism*. New Perspectives on the Past. Ithaca: Cornell University Press, 1983.

Gelvin, James L. *The Israel-Palestine Conflict: One Hundred Years of War*. Cambridge University Press, 2014. https://doi.org/10.1017/CBO9781139583824.

George, Alexander L. *Case Studies and Theory Development in the Social Sciences*. BCSIA Studies in International Security. Cambridge, Mass.: MIT Press, 2005.

Ghazzar, Brenda. "Politicians hope Doha agreement, Suleiman election will end violence." *The Jerusalem Post*, May 26, 2008. https://advance-lexis-com.proxy.bc.edu/api/document?collection=news&id=urn:contentItem:53Y6-YJH1-F12G-D55K-00000-00&context=1516831.

Gordon, Michael R., and Anthony Shadid. "U.S. Urges Iraqis to Try New Plan to Share Power." *The New York Times*, September 10, 2010.

https://www.nytimes.com/2010/09/10/world/middleeast/10policy.
html.

Graham, David A. "The Strange Friendship of Martin McGuinness and Ian Paisley." *The Atlantic*, March 21, 2017. https://www.theatlantic.com/international/archive/2017/03/martin-mcguinness-ian-paisley/520257/.

Groarke, Emer. "'Mission Impossible': Exploring the Viability of Power-Sharing as a Conflict-Resolution Tool in Syria." *International Journal of Conflict Management* 27, no. 1 (2016): 2–24. http://dx.doi.org/10.1108/IJCMA-12-2014-0090.

Gurr, Ted Robert. "Peoples Against States: Ethnopolitical Conflict and the Changing World System: 1994 Presidential Address." *International Studies Quarterly* 38, no. 3 (1994): 347–77. https://doi.org/10.2307/2600737.

Hanf, Theodor. *Coexistence in Wartime Lebanon: Decline of a State and Rise of a Nation*. London: Centre for Lebanese Studies in association with IBTauris, 1993.

"Hariri, Aoun Discuss Govt after Hiatus." *Daily Star, The (Beirut, Lebanon)*, December 7, 2020. Access World News. https://infoweb.newsbank.com/apps/news/document-view?p=AWNB&docref=news/17F39CC497E5D7F8.

Harris, William W. *Lebanon: A History, 600-2011*. Studies in Middle Eastern History (New York, N.Y.). New York: Oxford University Press, 2012.

Hartzell, Caroline A, and Matthew Hoddie. "Power Sharing and the Rule of Law in the Aftermath of Civil War." *International Studies Quarterly* 63, no. 3 (September 1, 2019): 641–53. https://doi.org/10.1093/isq/sqz023.

Hayward, Katy. "The 2019 General Election in Northern Ireland: The Rise of the Centre Ground?" *The Political Quarterly* 91, no. 1 (2020): 49–55. https://doi.org/10.1111/1467-923X.12835.

Ḥāzin al-, Farīd. *The Communal Pact of National Identities: The Making and Politics of the 1943 National Pact*. Papers on Lebanon 12. Oxford: Centre for Lebanese Studies, 1991.

Hennessey, Thomas. *A History of Northern Ireland, 1920-1996*. Dublin: Gill & Macmillan, 1997.

————. *The Northern Ireland Peace Process: Ending the Troubles?* Dublin: Gill & Macmillan, 2000.

Hermez, Sami. *War Is Coming: Between Past and Future Violence in Lebanon.* The Ethnography of Political Violence. Philadelphia: University of Pennsylvania Press, Inc, University of Pennsylvania Press, 2017.

Hiro, Dilip. *Lebanon: Fire and Embers : A History of the Lebanese Civil War.* New York: St. Martin's Press, 1993.

Hobsbawm, Eric. "Mass-Producing Traditions: Europe, 1870-1914." In *The Invention of Tradition*, 263–307. Cambridge and New York, 1983.

Hoddie, Matthew, and Caroline Hartzell. "Civil War Settlements and the Implementation of Military Power-Sharing Arrangements." *Journal of Peace Research* 40, no. 3 (May 1, 2003): 303–20. https://doi.org/10.11 77/0022343303040003004.

Hooghe, Marc, and Kris Deschouwer. "Veto Players and Electoral Reform in Belgium." *West European Politics* 34, no. 3 (May 1, 2011): 626–43. https://doi.org/10.1080/01402382.2011.555987.

Horowitz, Donald L. *Ethnic Groups in Conflict.* Berkeley: University of California Press, 1985.

"How Diversity Makes Us Smarter." *Greater Good.* Accessed March 26, 2021. https://greatergood.berkeley.edu/article/item/how_diversity_ makes_us_smarter.

"How Do You Translate 'Zeft'?" *ArabLit & ArabLit Quarterly.* Accessed February 27, 2021. https://arablit.org/2016/08/26/ how-do-you-translate-zeft/.

Hubbard, Ben. "Lebanon Prime Minister Charged With Negligence in Beirut Blast." *The New York Times*, December 10, 2020. https://www. nytimes.com/2020/12/10/world/middleeast/beirut-explosion-charges. html.

Hull, Robert H. *The Irish Triangle: Conflict in Northern Ireland.* Princeton Legacy Library. Princeton, New Jersey ; Guildford, England: Princeton University Press, 1976.

Husseini, Rola el-, and Ryan Crocker. "The Lebanese Political System: The Elite Pacts of 1943 and 1989." In *Pax Syriana*, 1–22. Elite Politics in Postwar Lebanon. Syracuse University Press, 2012. https://www.jstor. org/stable/j.ctt1j1nvk4.7.

"Ian Paisley: 'Never! Never! Never!' And Other Notable Quotes." *The Irish Times*. Accessed February 19, 2021. https://www.irishtimes.com/news/politics/ian-paisley-never-never-never-and-other-notable-quotes-1.1926880.

Ibrahim, Youssef M. "LEBANESE FACTIONS AGREE ON CHARTER TO RESOLVE STRIFE." *The New York Times*, October 23, 1989. https://www.nytimes.com/1989/10/23/world/lebanese-factions-agree-on-charter-to-resolve-strife.html.

Independent International Commission on Decommissioning (IICD) statement. September 26, 2005. https://cain.ulster.ac.uk/events/peace/decommission/iicd260905.pdf

"In Lebanon, a University Unites a Fragmented Society." Accessed February 15, 2021. https://www.chronicle.com/article/in-lebanon-a-university-unites-a-fragmented-society/.

Ipperciel, Donald. "Constitutional Democracy and Civic Nationalism." *Nations and Nationalism* 13, no. 3 (2007): 395–416. https://doi.org/10.1111/j.1469-8129.2007.00293.x.

"Is Beirut's Glitzy Downtown Redevelopment All That It Seems?" *The Guardian*, January 22, 2015. http://www.theguardian.com/cities/2015/jan/22/beirut-lebanon-glitzy-downtown-redevelopment-gucci-prada.

"Is Lebanon a Failed State? Here's What the Numbers Say." *Council on Foreign Relations*. Accessed January 4, 2021. https://www.cfr.org/in-brief/lebanon-failed-state-heres-what-numbers-say.

Joshi, Madhav, Jason Michael Quinn, and Patrick M Regan. "Annualized Implementation Data on Comprehensive Intrastate Peace Accords, 1989–2012." *Journal of Peace Research* 52, no. 4 (2015): 551–62. https://doi.org/10.1177/0022343314567486.

Kalyvas, Stathis N. "Wanton and Senseless?: The Logic of Massacres in Algeria." *Rationality and Society* 11, no. 3 (1999): 243–85. https://doi.org/10.1177/104346399011003001.

Kaufmann, Chiam. "Possible and Impossible Solutions to Ethnic Civil Wars." *International Security* 20, no. 4 (1996): 136–75.

———. "Rational Choice and Progress in the Study of Ethnic Conflict: A Review Essay." *Security Studies* 14, no. 1 (2005): 178–207. https://doi.org/10.1080/09636410591002554.

Kerr, Michael. *Imposing Power-Sharing :Conflict and Coexistence in Northern Ireland and Lebanon /*. Dublin ;, 2006. http://hdl.handle.net/2027/mdp.39015064694444.

Kotanidis, Silvia. "Understanding the d'Hondt Method." *European Parliamentary Research Service*, June 2019. https://www.europarl.europa.eu/RegData/etudes/BRIE/2019/637966/EPRS_BRI(2019)637966_EN.pdf.

"Labour Force Survey Religion Report 2017." *The Executive Office*, January 30, 2019. https://www.executiveoffice-ni.gov.uk/news/labour-force-survey-religion-report-2017.

"Lebanon – Arab Barometer." Accessed March 21, 2021. https://www.arabbarometer.org/countries/lebanon/.

"Lebanon's Civil War: Seven Lessons Forty Years On." *European Union Institute for Security Studies*. LU: Publications Office, 2015. https://data.europa.eu/doi/10.2815/475463.

"Lebanon vs. Connecticut (USA): Comparea Area Comparison." Accessed January 4, 2021. http://www.comparea.org/LBN+US_CT.

Lijphart, Arend "Consociational Democracy." In *The Oxford Companion to Comparative Politics*. Oxford University Press, 2012. https://www.oxfordreference.com/view/10.1093/acref/9780199738595.001.0001/acref-9780199738595-e-95.

———. *Democracy in Plural Societies: A Comparative Exploration*. New Haven: Yale University Press, 1977.

———. "Typologies of Democratic Systems." *Comparative Political Studies* 1, no. 1 (1969 1968): 3–44.

Majed, Rima. "What's So Deep About Deeply Divided Societies? Rethinking Sectarianism in the Middle East." American University of Beirut. Accessed February 27, 2021. http://www.aub.edu.lb:80/nyo/Briefings/Pages/sectarianismfulltextsummary.aspx.

Makdisi, Ussama Samir. *The Culture of Sectarianism: Community, History, and Violence in Nineteenth-Century Ottoman Lebanon*. Berkeley, Calif.: University of California Press, 2000.

Maktabi, Rania. "The Lebanese Census of 1932 Revisited. Who Are the Lebanese?" *British Journal of Middle Eastern Studies* 26, no. 2 (1999): 219–41.

"Mashrou' Leila: Lil Watan (نِطْوَلِل)." *Lebanese Arabic Institute*, December 4, 2016. https://www.lebanesearabicinstitute.com/mashrou-leila-lil-watan/.

May, Samantha. "The Rise of the 'Resistance Axis': Hezbollah and the Legacy of the Taif Agreement." *Nationalism and Ethnic Politics* 25, no. 1 (January 2, 2019): 115–32. https://doi.org/10.1080/13537113.2019.1565184.

McGarry, John. *Explaining Northern Ireland: Broken Images*. Oxford ; Cambridge, Mass.: Blackwell, 1995.

———. *The Northern Ireland Conflict: Consociational Engagements*. Oxford ; New York: Oxford University Press, 2004.

McGonagle, Suzanne. "Almost Equal Numbers of Catholics and Protestants in Northern Ireland of Working Age for the First Time." *The Irish News*, February 1, 2019. http://www.irishnews.com/news/northernirelandnews/2019/02/01/news/almost-equal-numbers-of-catholics-and-protestants-in-northern-ireland-of-working-age-for-the-first-time-1541284/.

McLoughlin, P. J. "'The First Major Step in the Peace Process'? Exploring the Impact of the Anglo-Irish Agreement on Irish Republican Thinking." *Irish Political Studies* 29, no. 1 (January 2, 2014): 116–33. https://doi.org/10.1080/07907184.2013.875895.

Mitchell, David. "Sticking to Their Guns? The Politics of Arms Decommissioning in Northern Ireland, 1998–2007." *Contemporary British History* 24, no. 3 (September 1, 2010): 341–61. https://doi.org/10.1080/13619462.2010.497253.

Moriarty, Gerry. "Northern Ireland: Polls Can Provide More Confusion than Clarity." *The Irish Times*. Accessed February 22, 2021. https://www.irishtimes.com/news/ireland/irish-news/northern-ireland-polls-can-provide-more-confusion-than-clarity-1.4344768.

———. "Shared Island: Northern Ireland Is Still a Society on a Sectarian Edge." *The Irish Times*. Accessed February 22, 2021. https://www.irishtimes.com/news/ireland/irish-news/shared-island-northern-ireland-is-still-a-society-on-a-sectarian-edge-1.4344699.

Morrissey, Sinéad. "Thoughts in a Black Taxi." In *There Was Fire In Vancouver*, 19–20. Manchester, United Kingdom: Carcanet Press

Ltd, 1996. https://www.proquest.com/docview/2148060035/
citation/8559F67403CE4A26PQ/13.

Mudd, Tom. "In Belfast, Cabs Offer Tours Showing Scenes of Conflict."
Wall Street Journal, May 24, 2002. https://www.wsj.com/articles/
SB1022159743471097240.

Nagle, John. "Ghosts, Memory, and the Right to the Divided City:
Resisting Amnesia in Beirut City Centre." *Antipode* 49, no. 1 (2017):
149–68. https://doi.org/10.1111/anti.12263.

"Nations and States." Accessed January 8, 2021. https://www.globalpolicy.
org/component/content/article/172-general/30345-nations-and-states.
html.

"New Report Reveals Substantial Demographic Changes in Lebanon."
annahar.com. Accessed March 21, 2021. https://www.annahar.com/
english/article/1002964-new-report-reveals-substantial-demographic-
changes-in-lebanon.

"NI Life and Times Survey - Political Attitudes." Accessed February 24,
2021. https://www.ark.ac.uk/nilt/results/polatt.html#identity.

Nora, Pierre. "Between Memory and History: Les Lieux de Mémoire."
Representations, no. 26 (1989): 7–24. https://doi.org/10.2307/2928520.

"Northern Ireland Assembly Elections 2003." Accessed March 15, 2021.
https://www.ark.ac.uk/elections/fa03.htm.

"Northern Ireland Peace Agreement (The Good Friday Agreement) | UN
Peacemaker." Accessed October 14, 2020. https://peacemaker.un.org/
uk-ireland-good-friday98.

"Northern Ireland Political Parties | Special Reports." *The Guardian*.
Accessed March 1, 2021. https://www.theguardian.com/politics/
northernirelandassembly/page/0,,1090664,00.html.

"Northern Ireland Poll Shows 45.4% Back Irish Unity and 46.8% Support
Union with UK." *Belfast Telegraph*. Accessed February 25, 2021.
https://www.belfasttelegraph.co.uk/news/northern-ireland/northern-
ireland-poll-shows-454-back-irish-unity-and-468-support-union-
with-uk-38989093.html.

"Northern Ireland: Restoration of the Power-Sharing
Executive," *The Institute for Government*. January 13, 2020.
https://www.instituteforgovernment.org.uk/explainers/
northern-ireland-restoration-power-sharing-executive.

"Northern Ireland: The Civil Rights Movement - CCEA - GCSE History Revision - CCEA." *BBC Bitesized*. Accessed March 5, 2021. https://www.bbc.co.uk/bitesize/guides/z3w2mp3/revision/2.

O'Kane, Eamonn. "Anglo–Irish Relations and the Northern Ireland Peace Process: From Exclusion to Inclusion." *Contemporary British History* 18, no. 1 (March 1, 2004): 78–99. https://doi.org/10.1080/13619460 42000217310.

"Omagh Bombing: Key Events before and after the Attack." *The Irish Times*. Accessed March 5, 2021. https://www.irishtimes.com/news/ireland/irish-news/omagh-bombing-key-events-before-and-after-the-attack-1.3593660.

Ommering, Erik van. "Schooling in Conflict: An Ethnographic Study from Lebanon." Edited by Madeleine Leonard, Martina McKnight, and Spyros Spyrou. *International Journal of Sociology and Social Policy* 31, no. 9/10 (January 1, 2011): 543–54. https://doi.org/10.1108/01443331111164133.

Osborne, R. D. "'Evidence' and Equality in Northern Ireland." *Evidence & Policy* 3, no. 1 (January 2007): 79–97. http://dx.doi.org/10.1332/174426407779702120.

Phillips, David L. "Power-Sharing in Iraq," *Council on Foreign Relations*, CRS No. 6, April, 2005.

"Poll Shows Northern Ireland Majority against United Ireland." *Reuters*, February 18, 2020. https://www.reuters.com/article/us-britain-nireland-poll-idUSKBN20C0WI.

Posen, Barry R. "The Security Dilemma and Ethnic Conflict." *Survival* 35, no. 1 (March 1, 1993): 27–47. https://doi.org/10.1080/00396339308442672.

Pospieszna, Paulina, and Gerald Schneider. "The Illusion of 'Peace Through Power-Sharing': Constitutional Choice in the Shadow of Civil War." *Civil Wars* 15, no. sup1 (December 4, 2013): 44–70. https://doi.org/10.1080/13698249.2013.850877.

"Protestant and Catholic Employment Rates Level for First Time in Northern Ireland." *Belfast Telegraph*. Accessed March 11, 2021. https://www.belfasttelegraph.co.uk/news/northern-ireland/protestant-and-catholic-employment-rates-level-for-first-time-in-northern-ireland-35398733.html.

"Protests in Lebanon as Local Currency Hits Record Low." *AP News*. Accessed March 4, 2021. https://apnews.com/article/lebanon-coronavirus-pandemic-financial-markets-syria-beirut-68f65031f2a98 7ca52f483c74e50593f.

Rafic Hariri - Charlie Rose. Accessed March 21, 2021. https://charlierose.com/videos/13778.

"Remarks by President Trump to the 72nd Session of the United Nations General Assembly." *The White House*. Accessed January 8, 2021. https://www.whitehouse.gov/briefings-statements/remarks-president-trump-72nd-session-united-nations-general-assembly/.

"Resolving the Issue of War Displacement in Lebanon | Forced Migration Review." Accessed February 18, 2021. https://www.fmreview.org/land-and-property-issues/assaf-elfil.

"Responsibility to Protect: A Short History." *Foreign Policy*. Accessed March 29, 2021. https://foreignpolicy.com/2011/10/11/responsibility-to-protect-a-short-history/.

Riches, Christopher, and Jan Palmowski. "St Andrews Agreement." In *A Dictionary of Contemporary World History*. Oxford University Press, 2019. https://www.oxfordreference.com/view/10.1093/acref/9780191870903.001.0001/acref-9780191870903-e-2676.

Roeder, Philip G., and Donald S. Rothchild. *Sustainable Peace: Power and Democracy after Civil Wars*. Ithaca: Cornell University Press, 2005.

"Roots of the Shi'i Movement." MERIP, June 24, 1985. https://merip.org/1985/06/roots-of-the-shii-movement/.

Rosiny, Stephan. "Power Sharing in Syria: Lessons from Lebanon's Taif Experience." *Middle East Policy* 20, no. 3 (2013): 41–55. https://doi.org/10.1111/mepo.12031.

Ruohomaki, Jyrki. "Parity of Esteem: A Conceptual Approach to the Northern Ireland Conflict." *Alternatives: Global, Local, Political* 35, no. 2 (April 1, 2010): 163–86.

Rushton, J. Philippe. "Ethnic Nationalism, Evolutionary Psychology and Genetic Similarity Theory." *Nations and Nationalism* 11, no. 4 (2005): 489–507. https://doi.org/10.1111/j.1469-8129.2005.00216.x.

Saliba, Issam. "Lebanon: Constitutional Law and the Political Rights of Religious Communities | Law Library of Congress." *Library of Congress*,

April 2012. https://www.loc.gov/law/help/lebanon/contitutional-law.php.

Savage, Robert J. *The BBC's "Irish Troubles": Television, Conflict and Northern Ireland*. Manchester: University Press, 2015.

Sawalha, Aseel. *Reconstructing Beirut: Memory and Space in a Postwar Arab City*. Austin: University of Texas Press, 2010. https://muse.jhu.edu/book/574.

Shuayb, Maha. "Education for Social Cohesion Attempts in Lebanon: Reflections on the 1994 and 2010 Education Reforms." *Education as Change* 20, no. 3 (2016): 225–42. https://doi.org/10.17159/1947-9417/2016/1531.

Smith, Anthony D. *The Ethnic Origins of Nations*. Oxford, UK : New York, NY, USA: BBlackwell, 1987.

Stefansson, Anders H. "Coffee after Cleansing?: Co-Existence, Co-Operation, and Communication in Post-Conflict Bosnia and Herzegovina." *Focaal* 2010, no. 57 (2010): 62–76. https://doi.org/10.3167/fcl.2010.570105.

"Stormont Talks: Main NI Parties Agree Power-Sharing Deal." *BBC News*, January 10, 2020. https://www.bbc.com/news/uk-northern-ireland-51068774.

"Summary: Governing without Ministers," *The Institute for Government*. September 25, 2019. https://www.instituteforgovernment.org.uk/summary-governing-without-ministers-northern-ireland.

Suzanne Daley. "No Bridging Language Divide; Tensions Run Higher than Ever between Belgium's Two Halves." *National Post (Toronto)*. 2010.

"Taif Accords | UN Peacemaker." Accessed January 4, 2021. https://peacemaker.un.org/lebanon-taifaccords89.

Tamir, Yael. "Not So Civic: Is There a Difference Between Ethnic and Civic Nationalism?" *Annual Review of Political Science* 22, no. 1 (2019): 419–34. https://doi.org/10.1146/annurev-polisci-022018-024059.

Ṭarābulsī, Fawwāz. *A History of Modern Lebanon*. Second edition. New York, NY, London: Palgrave Macmillian, Pluto Press, 2012.

Tfaily, Rania, Hassan Diab, and Andrzej Kulczycki. "Educational Disparities and Conflict: Evidence from Lebanon." *Research in*

Comparative and International Education 8, no. 1 (March 1, 2013): 55–73. https://doi.org/10.2304/rcie.2013.8.1.55.

Tichborne, Henry. *A Letter of Sir Henry Tichborne to His Lady, of the Siege of Drogheda; and Other Passages of the Wars of Ireland Where He Commanded.* Eighteenth Century ; Reel 11081, No. 14. Drogheda: printed by John Fleming, 1772.

"The Belfast Agreement." *Gov.uk.* Accessed March 4, 2021. https://www.gov.uk/government/publications/the-belfast-agreement.

"The Cranberries – Zombie." Accessed March 9, 2021. https://genius.com/The-cranberries-zombie-lyrics.

"The Peace Walls of Belfast: Do They Still Help Keep the Peace?" *CBC,* August 29, 2019. https://www.cbc.ca/radio/ideas/the-peace-walls-of-belfast-do-they-still-help-keep-the-peace-1.5262640.

"The Cure of Troy." *Pittsburgh Post-Gazette.* Accessed March 24, 2021. https://www.post-gazette.com/news/insight/2021/02/21/The-cure-of-Troy/stories/202102210026.

"The Garden Of The Prophet by Kahlil Gibran." Accessed February 24, 2021. http://gutenberg.net.au/ebooks05/0500581h.html.

"The Lebanese Constitution." *Arab Law Quarterly* 12, no. 2 (1997): 224–61.

"The Northern Ireland Peace Process." *Council on Foreign Relations.* Accessed February 22, 2021. https://www.cfr.org/backgrounder/northern-ireland-peace-process.

"The Tourist Economy in Northern Ireland | Nibusinessinfo.Co.Uk." Accessed March 4, 2021. https://www.nibusinessinfo.co.uk/content/tourist-economy-northern-ireland.

Tonge, Jonathan. "The Impact and Consequences of Brexit for Northern Ireland." *European Parliament.* https://www.europarl.europa.eu/RegData/etudes/BRIE/2017/583116/IPOL_BRI%282017%29583116_EN.pdf.

Tonge, Jonathan, and Raul Gomez. "Shared Identity and the End of Conflict? How Far Has a Common Sense of 'Northern Irishness' Replaced British or Irish Allegiances since the 1998 Good Friday Agreement?" *Irish Political Studies* 30, no. 2 (April 3, 2015): 276–98. https://doi.org/10.1080/07907184.2015.1023716.

"Tourism | Department for the Economy," May 17, 2015. https://www.economy-ni.gov.uk/topics/tourism.

"Uber Has Met Its Match with Lebanon's Old-School Carpool Taxis." *The World from PRX*. Accessed February 26, 2021. https://www.pri.org/stories/2017-11-03/city-s-cheap-old-school-carpool-service-puts-uber-test.

Ulrichsen, Kristian Coates. "Consociationalism." In *A Dictionary of Politics in the Middle East*. Oxford University Press, 2018. https://www.oxfordreference.com/view/10.1093/acref/9780191835278.001.0001/acref-9780191835278-e-85.

Ulster's Solemn League and Covenant : Being Convinced in Our Consciences That Home Rule Would Be Disastrous to the Material Well-Being of Ulster as Well as of the Whole of Ireland... /. s.n., 1912.

Vaughan, Kenneth. "Who Benefits from Consociationalism? Religious Disparities in Lebanon's Political System." *Religions* 9, no. 2 (February 2018): 51. https://doi.org/10.3390/rel9020051.

Wee, Lionel. *The Singlish Controversy: Language, Culture and Identity in a Globalizing World*. Cambridge: Cambridge University Press, 2018. https://doi.org/10.1017/9781316855331.

Weidmann, Nils B., and Idean Salehyan. "Violence and Ethnic Segregation: A Computational Model Applied to Baghdad." *International Studies Quarterly* 57, no. 1 (March 1, 2013): 52–64. https://doi.org/10.1111/isqu.12059.

"What is the Northern Ireland Life and Times Survey?" *UK Data Archive Study Number 4767 – Northern Ireland Life and Times Survey, 2002.* https://sp.ukdataservice.ac.uk/doc/4767/mrdoc/pdf/4767userguide.pdf

"What Is the St Andrews Agreement?" *The Guardian*, October 17, 2006. http://www.theguardian.com/politics/2006/oct/17/northernireland.devolution1.

Wimmer, Andreas. *Facing Ethnic Conflicts: Toward a New Realism*. Lanham, MD: Rowman & Littlefield Publishers, 2004.

Winslow, Charles. *Lebanon: War and Politics in a Fragmented Society*. London; New York: Routledge, 1996.

Wolff, Stefan. "Consociationalism, Power Sharing, and Politics at the Center." Oxford Research Encyclopedia of International Studies, March 1, 2010. https://doi.org/10.1093/acrefore/9780190846626.013.65.

Wong, Lloyd. "Multiculturalism and Ethnic Pluralism in Sociology." In *Revisiting Multiculturalism in Canada: Theories, Policies and Debates*, edited by Shibao Guo and Lloyd Wong, 69–90. Rotterdam: SensePublishers, 2015. https://doi.org/10.1007/978-94-6300-208-0_5.

Yassin, Nasser. "Beirut." *Cities* 29, no. 1 (February 1, 2012): 64–73. https://doi.org/10.1016/j.cities.2011.02.001.